Learning
Regular
Expressions

The Pearson Addison-Wesley Learning Series

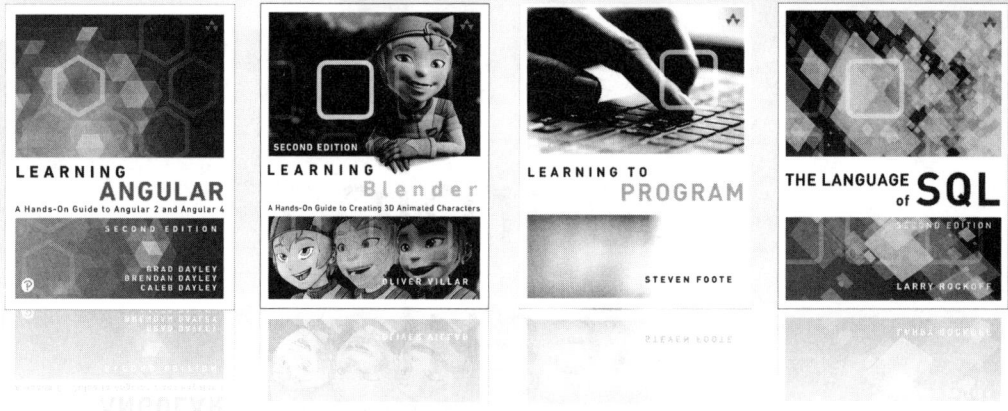

LEARNING ANGULAR
A Hands-On Guide to Angular 2 and Angular 4
SECOND EDITION
BRAD DAYLEY
BRENDAN DAYLEY
CALEB DAYLEY

LEARNING Blender
SECOND EDITION
A Hands-On Guide to Creating 3D Animated Characters
OLIVER VILLAR

LEARNING TO PROGRAM
STEVEN FOOTE

THE LANGUAGE of SQL
SECOND EDITION
LARRY ROCKOFF

Visit **informit.com/learningseries** for a complete list of available publications.

The **Pearson Addison-Wesley Learning Series** is a collection of hands-on programming guides that help you quickly learn a new technology or language so you can apply what you've learned right away.

Each title comes with sample code for the application or applications built in the text. This code is fully annotated and can be reused in your own projects with no strings attached. Many chapters end with a series of exercises to encourage you to reexamine what you have just learned, and to tweak or adjust the code as a way of learning.

Titles in this series take a simple approach: they get you going right away and leave you with the ability to walk off and build your own application and apply the language or technology to whatever you are working on.

Make sure to connect with us!
informit.com/socialconnect

Pearson
Addison-Wesley

informIT.com
the trusted technology learning source

O'REILLY
Safari

Learning
Regular
Expressions

Ben Forta

✦✦ Addison-Wesley

Boston • Columbus • Indianapolis • New York • San Francisco • Amsterdam
Cape Town • Dubai • London • Madrid • Milan • Munich • Paris
Montreal • Toronto • Delhi • Mexico City • São Paulo • Sidney
Hong Kong • Seoul • Singapore • Taipei • Tokyo

Learning Regular Expressions

For information about buying this title in bulk quantities, or for special sales opportunities (which may include electronic versions; custom cover designs; and content particular to your business, training goals, marketing focus, or branding interests), please contact our corporate sales department at corpsales@pearsoned.com or (800) 382-3419.

For government sales inquiries, please contact governmentsales@pearsoned.com.

For questions about sales outside the U.S., please contact intlcs@pearson.com.

Visit us on the Web: informit.com/aw

Library of Congress Control Number: 2018935165

ISBN-13: 978-0-13-475706-3
ISBN-10: 0-13-475706-8

1   18

Editor
Mark Taber

Managing Editor
Sandra Schroeder

Senior Project Editor
Tonya Simpson

Copy Editor
Bill McManus

Technical Editor
Ben Schupak

Indexer
Erika Millen

Compositor
codemantra

Proofreader
Jeanine Furino

Cover Designer
Chuti Prasertsith

Contents at a Glance

Table of Contents

About the Author

Ben Forta is Adobe Systems' Senior Director of Education Initiatives. He is also the author of numerous books on SQL, regular expressions, ColdFusion, Windows development, JSP, and more. His book *Teach Yourself SQL in 10 Minutes* is the best-selling book on SQL of all time.

Accessing the Free Web Edition

Your purchase of this book in any format includes access to the corresponding Web Edition, which provides several special online-only features:

- The complete text of the book

- Links to online regular expression testers

- Updates and corrections as they become available

The Web Edition can be viewed on all types of computers and mobile devices with any modern web browser that supports HTML5.

To get access to the *Learning Regular Expressions* Web Edition all you need to do is register this book:

1. Go to www.informit.com/register.

2. Sign in or create a new account.

3. Enter the ISBN: 9780134757063.

4. Answer the questions as proof of purchase.

5. The Web Edition will appear under the Digital Purchases tab on your Account page. Click the Launch link to access the product.

Introduction

Regular expressions and the regular expression language have been around for many years. Regular expression experts have long been armed with an incredibly powerful tool, one that can be used to perform all sorts of powerful text processing and manipulation in just about every language and on every platform.

That's the good news. The bad news is that for too long, regular expressions have been the exclusive property of only the most tech savvy. Most of us do not fully understand what regular expressions do and what problems they solve. And those who have braved them find regular expression syntax to be unintuitive, and even convoluted at times. That's sad, because the truth is that regular expressions are nowhere near as complex as they appear to be at first glance. All it takes is a clear understanding of the problem being solved and how to leverage regular expressions so as to solve them.

Part of the problem is the scarcity of quality content on the subject. The few books on regular expressions (and indeed, most of the Web sites boasting regular expression tutorials) tend to concentrate on the syntax, defining what { does and how + differs from *. But that is the easy part; there are not that many special characters in the regular expression language. The tricky part is understanding how they should be used so as to solve real-world problems.

The book you are holding is not intended to be the last word on everything there is to know about regular expressions. If that is what you want, you'll need a copy of Jeffrey Friedl's *Mastering Regular Expressions* (O'Reilly, ISBN 0596528124). Mr. Friedl is the acknowledged regular expressions guru, and his book is the definitive and most comprehensive on the subject. But, and no offense to Mr. Friedl, his book is not for beginners—or even for casual users who just want to get their jobs done without needing to understand the inner workings of regular expression engines. Not that it is not useful information—it is, but not when all you want to do is add validation to your HTML forms or simply perform powerful replace operations on parsed text. If you need to get up and running quickly using regular expressions, you'll find yourself torn between having too little information to be productive and having too much information to know where to begin.

And that is where this book comes in. *Learning Regular Expressions* will teach you the regular expressions that you really need to know, starting with simple text matches and working up to more complex topics, including the use of backreferences, conditional evaluation, and look-ahead processing. You'll learn what you can use, and you'll learn it methodically, systematically, and simply by using clear and practical examples and solving real problems.

Who Is *Learning Regular Expressions* For?

This book is for you if:

- You are new to regular expressions.

- You want to quickly learn how to get the most out of the regular expression language.

- You want to gain an edge by learning to solve real problems using one of the most powerful (and least understood) tools available to you.

- You build Web applications and crave more sophisticated form and text processing.

- You use JavaScript, Java, .NET, PHP, Python, MySQL, (and any other languages and DBMSs with regular expression support), and you want to learn how to use regular expressions within your own application development.

- You want to be productive quickly and easily in regular expressions, without having to call someone for help.

So turn to Lesson 1, "Introducing Regular Expressions," and get to work. You'll be leveraging the power of regular expressions in no time at all and wondering how you ever managed without them.

Lesson 1

Introducing Regular Expressions

In this lesson you'll learn what regular expressions are and what they can do for you.

Understanding the Need

Regular expressions (often shortened as *RegEx* or *regex*) are tools, and like all tools, regular expressions are designed to solve a very specific problem. The best way to understand regular expressions and what they do is to understand the problem they solve.

Consider the following scenarios:

- You are searching for a file containing the text car (regardless of case) but do not want to also locate car in the middle of a word (for example, scar, carry, and incarcerate).

- You are generating a Web page and need to display text retrieved from a database. Text may contain URLs, and you want those URLs to be clickable in the generated page (so that instead of generating just text, you generate a valid HTML <a href></a>).

- You create an app with a form that prompts for user information including e-mail address. You need to verify that specified addresses are formatted correctly (that they are syntactically valid).

- You are editing source code and need to replace all occurrences of size with iSize, but only size and not size as part of another word.

- You are displaying a list of all files in your computer file system and want to filter so that you locate only files containing the text Application.

- You are importing data into an application. The data is tab delimited and your application supports CSV format files (one row per line, comma-delimited values, each possibly enclosed with quotes).

- You need to search a file for some specific text, but only at a specific location (perhaps at the start of a line or at the end of a sentence).

All these scenarios present unique programming challenges. And all of them can be solved in just about any language that supports conditional processing and string manipulation. But how complex a task would the solution become? You would need to loop through words or characters one at a time, perform all sorts of if statement tests, track lots of flags so as to know what you had found and what you had not, check for whitespace and special characters, and more. And you would need to do it all manually, over and over.

Or you could use regular expressions. Each of the preceding challenges can be solved using well-crafted statements—highly concise strings containing text and special instructions—statements that may look like this:

`\b[Cc][Aa][Rr]\b`

> **Note**
> Don't worry if the previous line does not make sense yet; it will shortly.

How Regular Expressions Are Used

Look at the problem scenarios again and you will notice that they all fall into one of two types: either information is being located (search) or information is being located and edited (replace). In fact, at its simplest, that is all that regular expressions are ever used for: search and replace. Every regular expression either matches text (performing a search) or matches and replaces text (performing a replace).

RegEx Searches

Regular expressions are used in searches when the text to be searched for is highly dynamic, as in searching for `car` in the scenario described earlier. For starters, you need to locate `car` or `CAR` or `Car` or even `CaR`; that's the easy part (many search tools are capable of performing searches that are not case sensitive). The trickier part is ensuring that `scar`, `carry`, and `incarcerate` are not matched. Some more sophisticated editors have *Match Only Whole Word* options, but many don't, and you may not be making this change in a document you are editing. Using a regular expression for the search, instead of just the text `car`, solves the problem.

> **Tip**
> Want to know what the solution to this one is? You've actually seen it already—it is the sample statement shown previously, `\b[Cc][Aa][Rr]\b`.

It is worth noting that testing for equality (for example, *does this user-specified e-mail address match this regular expression*) is a search operation. The entire user-provided string is being searched for a match (in contrast to a substring search, which is what searches usually are).

RegEx Replaces

Regular expression searches are immensely powerful, very useful, and not that difficult to learn. As such, many of the lessons and examples that you will run into are matches. However, the real power of regex is seen in replace operations, such as in the earlier scenario in which you replace URLs with clickable URLs. For starters, this requires that you be able to locate URLs within text (perhaps searching for strings that start with `http://` or `https://` and ending with a period or a comma or whitespace). Then it also requires that you replace the found URL with two occurrences of the matched string with embedded HTML so that:

```
http://www.forta.com/
```

is replaced with

```
<a href="http://www.forta.com">http://www.forta.com/</a>
```

Or perhaps the text being located is just an address, and not a fully qualified URL, like this:

```
www.forta.com
```

which would also need to be turned into

```
<a href="http://www.forta.com">http://www.forta.com/</a>
```

The Search and Replace option in most applications could not handle this type of replace operation, but this task is incredibly easy using a regular expression.

So What Exactly Is a Regular Expression?

Now that you know what regular expressions are used for, a definition is in order. Simply put, *regular expressions* are strings that are used to match and manipulate text. Regular expressions are created using the regular expression language, a specialized language designed to do everything that was just discussed and more. Like any language, regular expressions have a specific syntax and instructions that you must learn, and that is what this book will teach you.

The regular expression language is not a full programming language. It is usually not even an actual program or utility that you can install and use. More often than not, regular expressions are mini-languages built-in to other languages or products. The good news is that just about any decent language or tool these days supports regular expressions. The bad news is that the regular expression language itself is not going to look anything like the language or tool you are using it with. The regular expression language is a language unto itself—and not the most intuitive or obvious language at that.

> **Note**
>
> Regular expressions originate from research in the 1950s in the field of mathematics. Years later, the principles and ideas derived from this early work made their way into the Unix world into the Perl language and utilities such as `grep`. For many years, regular expressions (used in the scenarios previously described) were the exclusive domain of the Unix community, but this has changed, and now regular expressions are supported in a variety of forms on just about every computing platform.

To put all this into perspective, the following are all valid regular expressions (and all will make sense shortly):

- `Ben`
- `.`
- `www\.forta\.com`
- `[a-zA-Z0-9_.]*`
- `<[Hh]1>.*</[Hh]1>`
- `\r\n\r\n`
- `\d{3,3}-\d{3,3}-\d{4,4}`

It is important to note that syntax is the easiest part of mastering regular expressions. The real challenge, however, is learning how to apply that syntax, how to dissect problems into solvable regex solutions. That is something that cannot be taught by simply reading a book, but like any language, mastery comes with practice.

Using Regular Expressions

As previously explained, there is no regular expressions program; it is not an application you run nor software you buy or download. Rather, the regular expressions language is implemented in lots of software products, languages, utilities, and development environments.

How regular expressions are used and how regular expression functionality is exposed varies from one application to the next. Some applications have menu options and dialog boxes used to access regular expressions, whereas programming languages typically provide functions or classes or objects that expose regex functionality.

Furthermore, not all regular expression implementations are the same. There are often subtle (and sometimes not so subtle) differences between syntax and features.

Appendix A, "Regular Expressions in Popular Applications and Languages," provides usage details and notes for many of the applications and languages that support regular expressions. Before you proceed to the next lesson, consult that appendix to learn the specifics pertaining to the application or language that you will be using.

To help you get started quickly, you'll find links to online regular expression testing tools on this book's Web page at

```
http://forta.com/books/0134757068/
```

These online tools are often the simplest way to experiment with regular expressions.

Before You Get Started

Before you go any further, take note of a couple of important points:

- When using regular expressions, you will discover that there are almost always multiple solutions to any problem. Some may be simpler, some may be faster, some may be more portable, and some may be more capable. There is rarely a right or wrong solution when writing regular expressions (as long as your solution works, of course).

- As already stated, differences exist between regex implementations. As much as possible, the examples and lessons used in this book apply to all major implementations, and differences or incompatibilities are noted as such.

- As with any language, the key to learning regular expressions is practice, practice, practice.

Note
I strongly suggest that you try each and every example as you work through this book.

Summary

Regular expressions are one of the most powerful tools available for text manipulation. The regular expressions language is used to construct regular expressions (the actual constructed string is called a *regular expression*), and regular expressions are used to perform both search and replace operations.

Lesson 2
Matching Single Characters

In this lesson you'll learn how to perform simple character matches of one or more characters.

Matching Literal Text

Ben is a regular expression. Because it is plain text, it may not look like a regular expression, but it is. Regular expressions can contain plain text (and may even contain *only* plain text). Admittedly, this is a total waste of regular expression processing, but it's a good place to start.

So, here goes:

Text

```
Hello, my name is Ben. Please visit
my website at http://www.forta.com/.
```

RegEx

```
Ben
```

Result

```
Hello, my name is Ben. Please visit
my website at http://www.forta.com/.
```

Analysis

The regular expression used here is literal text and it matches Ben in the original text.

> **Note**
>
> In the examples you'll see that the matched text is shaded. We'll use this format throughout the book so you can easily see exactly what an example matched.

Let's look at another example using the same search text and a different regular expression:

Text

```
Hello, my name is Ben. Please visit
my website at http://www.forta.com/.
```

RegEx

```
my
```

Result

Hello, `my` name is Ben. Please visit
`my` website at http://www.forta.com/.

Analysis

my is also static text, but notice how two occurrences of my were matched.

How Many Matches?

The default behavior of most regular expression engines is to return just the first match. In the preceding example, the first my would typically be a match, but not the second.

So why were two matches made? Most regex implementations provide a mechanism by which to obtain a list of all matches (usually returned in an array or some other special format). In JavaScript, for example, using the optional g (global) flag returns an array containing all the matches.

> **Note**
>
> Consult Appendix A, "Regular Expressions in Popular Applications and Languages," to learn how to perform global matches in your language or tool.

Handling Case Sensitivity

Regular expressions are case sensitive, so Ben will not match ben. However, most regex implementations also support matches that are not case sensitive. JavaScript users, for example, can specify the optional i flag to force a search that is not case sensitive.

> **Note**
>
> Consult Appendix A to learn how to use your language or tool to perform searches that are not case sensitive.

Matching Any Characters

The regular expressions thus far have matched static text only—rather anticlimactic, indeed. Next we'll look at matching unknown characters.

In regular expressions, special characters (or sets of characters) are used to identify what is to be searched for. The `.` character (period, or full stop) matches any one character.

Therefore, searching for `c.t` will match `cat` and `cot` (and a bunch of other nonsensical words, too).

Here is an example:

Text

```
sales1.xls
orders3.xls
sales2.xls
sales3.xls
apac1.xls
europe2.xls
na1.xls
na2.xls
sa1.xls
```

RegEx

```
sales.
```

Result

```
sales1.xls
orders3.xls
sales2.xls
sales3.xls
apac1.xls
europe2.xls
na1.xls
na2.xls
sa1.xls
```

Analysis

Here the regex `sales.` is being used to find all filenames starting with `sales` and followed by another character. Three of the nine files match the pattern.

> **Tip**
>
> You'll often see the term *pattern* used to describe the actual regular expression.

> **Note**
>
> Notice that regular expressions match patterns with string contents. Matches will not always be entire strings, but the characters that match a pattern—even if they are only part of a string. In the example used here, the regular expression did not match a filename; rather, it matched part of a filename. This distinction is important to remember when passing the results of a regular expression to some other code or application for processing.

. matches any character, alphabetic characters, digits, and even . itself:

Text

```
sales.xls
sales1.xls
orders3.xls
sales2.xls
sales3.xls
apac1.xls
europe2.xls
na1.xls
na2.xls
sa1.xls
```

RegEx

```
sales.
```

Result

```
sales.xls
sales1.xls
orders3.xls
sales2.xls
sales3.xls
apac1.xls
europe2.xls
na1.xls
na2.xls
sa1.xls
```

Analysis

This example contains one additional file, sales.xls. The file was matched by the pattern sales. as . matches any character.

Multiple instances of . may be used, either together (one after the other—using .. will match any two characters next to each other) or in different locations in the pattern.

Let's look at another example using the same text. This time you need to find all files for North America (na) or South America (sa) regardless of what digit comes next:

Text

```
sales1.xls
orders3.xls
sales2.xls
sales3.xls
apac1.xls
europe2.xls
na1.xls
na2.xls
sa1.xls
```

RegEx

```
.a.
```

Result

```
sales1.xls
orders3.xls
sales2.xls
sales3.xls
apac1.xls
europe2.xls
na1.xls
na2.xls
sa1.xls
```

Analysis

The regex `.a.` did indeed find na1, na2, and sa1, but it also found four other matches that it was not supposed to. Why? Because the pattern matches any three characters so long as the middle one is a.

What is needed is a pattern that matches `.a.` followed by a period. Here is another try:

Text

```
sales1.xls
orders3.xls
sales2.xls
sales3.xls
apac1.xls
europe2.xls
na1.xls
na2.xls
sa1.xls
```

RegEx

```
.a..
```

Result

```
sales1.xls
orders3.xls
sales2.xls
sales3.xls
apac1.xls
europe2.xls
na1.xls
na2.xls
sa1.xls
```

Analysis

`.a..` does not work any better than `.a.` did; appending a `.` will match any additional character (regardless of what it is). How then can you search for `.` when `.` is a special character that
matches any character?

Matching Special Characters

A `.` has a special meaning in regex. If you need a `.` in your pattern, you need a way to tell regex
that you want the actual `.` character and not the regex special meaning of the `.` character. To
do this, you escape the `.` by preceding it with a `\` (backslash). `\` is a *metacharacter* (a fancy way of
saying *a character with a special meaning, in contrast to the character itself*). Therefore, `.` means match
any character, and `\.` means match the `.` character itself.

Let's try the previous example again, this time escaping the `.` with `\.`:

Text

```
sales1.xls
orders3.xls
sales2.xls
sales3.xls
apac1.xls
europe2.xls
na1.xls
na2.xls
sa1.xls
```

RegEx

```
.a.\.
```

Result

```
sales1.xls
orders3.xls
sales2.xls
sales3.xls
apac1.xls
europe2.xls
na1.xls
na2.xls
sa1.xls
```

Analysis

.a.\. did the trick. The first . matched n (in the first two matches) or s (in the third). The second . matched 1 (in the first and third matches) or 2 (in the second). \. then matched the . separating the filename from the extension.

The example could be further improved by including the xls in the pattern so as to prevent a filename such as sa3.doc from being matched, like this:

Text

```
sales1.xls
orders3.xls
sales2.xls
sales3.xls
apac1.xls
europe2.xls
na1.xls
na2.xls
sa1.xls
```

RegEx

```
.a.\.xls
```

Result

```
sales1.xls
orders3.xls
sales2.xls
sales3.xls
apac1.xls
europe2.xls
na1.xls
na2.xls
sa1.xls
```

In regular expressions, \ is always used to mark the beginning of a block of one or more characters that have a special meaning. You saw \. here, and you'll see many more examples of using \ in future lessons.

> **Note**
>
> The use of special characters is covered in Lesson 4, "Using Metacharacters."

> **Note**
>
> In case you were wondering, to escape \ (so as to search for a backslash) use \\ (two backslashes).

> **Tip**
>
> . matches all characters, right? Well, maybe not. In most regular expression implementations, . matches every character except a newline character.

Summary

Regular expressions, also called patterns, are strings made up of characters. These characters may be literal (actual text) or metacharacters (special characters with special meanings), and in this lesson you learned how to match a single character using both literal text and metacharacters. . matches any character. \ is used to escape characters and to start special character sequences.

Lesson 3

Matching Sets of Characters

In this lesson you'll learn how to work with sets of characters. Unlike the ., which matches any single character (as you learned in the previous lesson), sets enable you to match specific characters and character ranges.

Matching One of Several Characters

As you learned in the previous lesson, . matches any one character (as does any literal character). In the final example in that lesson, .a was used to match both na and sa, . matched both the n and s. But what if there was a file (containing Canadian sales data) named ca1.xls as well, and you still wanted to match only na and sa)? . would also match c, and so that filename would also be matched.

Text

```
sales1.xls
orders3.xls
sales2.xls
sales3.xls
apac1.xls
europe2.xls
na1.xls
na2.xls
sa1.xls
ca1.xls
```

RegEx

```
.a.\.xls
```

Result

```
sales1.xls
orders3.xls
sales2.xls
sales3.xls
apac1.xls
europe2.xls
na1.xls
na2.xls
sa1.xls
ca1.xls
```

To find n or s you would not want to match *any* character, you would want to match just those two characters. In regular expressions a set of characters is defined using the metacharacters [and]. [and] define a character set, everything between them is part of the set, and any one of the set members must match (but not all).

Here is a revised version of that example from the previous lesson:

Text

```
sales1.xls
orders3.xls
sales2.xls
sales3.xls
apac1.xls
europe2.xls
na1.xls
na2.xls
sa1.xls
ca1.xls
```

RegEx

```
[ns]a.\.xls
```

Result

```
sales1.xls
orders3.xls
sales2.xls
sales3.xls
apac1.xls
europe2.xls
na1.xls
na2.xls
sa1.xls
ca1.xls
```

Analysis

The regular expression used here starts with `[ns]`; this matches either n or s (but not c or any other character). The opening `[` and closing `]` do not match any characters—they define the set. The literal `a` matches a, `.` matches any character, `\.` matches the ., and the literal `xls` matches xls. When you use this pattern, only the three desired filenames are matched.

> **Note**
>
> Actually, `[ns]a.\.xls` is not quite right either. If a file named `usa1.xls` existed, it would match, too (the opening u would be ignored and `sa1.xls` would match). The solution to this problem involves position matching, which will be covered in Lesson 6, "Position Matching."

> **Tip**
>
> As you can see, testing regular expressions can be tricky. Verifying that a pattern matches what you want is pretty easy. The real challenge is in verifying that you are not also getting matches that you don't want.

Character sets are frequently used to make searches (or specific parts thereof) not case sensitive. For example:

Text

```
The phrase "regular expression" is often
abbreviated as RegEx or regex.
```

RegEx

```
[Rr]eg[Ee]x
```

Result

```
The phrase "regular expression" is often
abbreviated as RegEx or regex.
```

Analysis

The pattern used here contains two character sets: `[Rr]` matches R and r, and `[Ee]` matches E and e. This way, RegEx and regex are both matched. REGEX, however, would not match.

> **Tip**
>
> If you are using matching that is not case sensitive, this technique would be unnecessary. This type of matching is used only when performing case-sensitive searches that are partially not case sensitive.

Using Character Set Ranges

Let's take a look at the file list example again. The last used pattern, `[ns]a.\.xls`, has another problem. What if a file was named `sam.xls`? It, too, would be matched because the `.` matches all characters, not just digits.

Character sets can solve this problem as follows:

Text

```
sales1.xls
orders3.xls
sales2.xls
sales3.xls
apac1.xls
europe2.xls
sam.xls
na1.xls
na2.xls
sa1.xls
ca1.xls
```

RegEx

```
[ns]a[0123456789]\.xls
```

Result

```
sales1.xls
orders3.xls
sales2.xls
sales3.xls
apac1.xls
europe2.xls
sam.xls
na1.xls
na2.xls
sa1.xls
ca1.xls
```

Analysis

In this example, the pattern has been modified so that the first character would have to be either n or s, the second character would have to be a, and the third could be any digit (specified as `[0123456789]`). Notice that file `sam.xls` was not matched, because m did not match the list of allowed characters (the 10 digits).

When working with regular expressions, you will find that you frequently specify ranges of characters (0 through 9, A through z, and so on). To simplify working with character ranges, regex provides a special metacharacter: - (hyphen) is used to specify a range.

Following is the same example, this time using a range:

Text

```
sales1.xls
orders3.xls
sales2.xls
sales3.xls
apac1.xls
europe2.xls
sam.xls
na1.xls
na2.xls
sa1.xls
ca1.xls
```

RegEx

```
[ns]a[0-9]\.xls
```

Result

```
sales1.xls
orders3.xls
sales2.xls
sales3.xls
apac1.xls
europe2.xls
sam.xls
na1.xls
na2.xls
sa1.xls
ca1.xls
```

Analysis

Pattern [0-9] is functionally equivalent to [0123456789], and so the results are identical to those in the previous example.

Ranges are not limited to digits. The following are all valid ranges:

- A-Z matches all uppercase characters from A to Z.

- a-z matches all lowercase characters from a to z.

- A-F matches only uppercase characters A to F.

- A-z matches all characters between ASCII A to ASCII z (you should probably never use this pattern, because it also includes characters such as [and ^, which fall between z and a in the ASCII table).

Any two ASCII characters may be specified as the range start and end. In practice, however, ranges are usually made up of some or all digits and some or all alphabetic characters.

> **Tip**
>
> When you use ranges, be careful not to provide an end range that is less than the start range (like [3-1]). This will not work, and it will often prevent the entire pattern from working.

> **Note**
>
> - (hyphen) is a special metacharacter because it is only a metacharacter when used between [and]. Outside of a set, - is a literal and will match only -. As such, - does not need to be escaped.

Multiple ranges may be combined in a single set. For example, the following pattern matches any alphanumeric character in uppercase or lowercase, but not anything that is neither a digit nor an alphabetic character:

```
[A-Za-z0-9]
```

This pattern is shorthand for

```
[ABCDEFGHIJKLMNOPQRSTUVWXYZabcde
➥fghijklmnopqrstuvwxyz01234567890]
```

As you can see, ranges make regex syntax much cleaner.

Following is one more example, this time finding RGB values (colors specified in a hexadecimal notation representing the amount of red, green, and blue used to create the color). In Web pages, RGB values are specified as #000000 (black), #ffffff (white), #ff0000 (red), and so on. RGB values may be specified in uppercase or lowercase, and so #FF00ff (magenta) is legal, too. Here is an example taken from a CSS file:

Text

```
body {
    background-color: #fefbd8;
}
h1 {
    background-color: #0000ff;
}
div {
    background-color: #d0f4e6;
}
span {
    background-color: #f08970;
}
```

RegEx

```
#[0-9A-Fa-f][0-9A-Fa-f][0-9A-Fa-f][0-9A-Fa-f][0-9A-Fa-f][0-9A-Fa-f]
```

Result

```
body {
    background-color: #fefbd8;
}
h1 {
    background-color: #0000ff;
}
div {
    background-color: #d0f4e6;
}
span {
    background-color: #f08970;
}
```

Analysis

The pattern used here contains # as literal text and then the character set [0-9A-Fa-f]
repeated six times. This matches # followed by six characters, each of which must be
a digit or A through F (in either uppercase or lowercase).

"Anything But" Matching

Character sets are usually used to specify a list of characters of which any must match. But
occasionally, you'll want the reverse—a list of characters that you don't want to match. In
other words, *anything but the list specified here*.

Rather than having to enumerate every character you want (which could get rather lengthy
if you want all but a few), character sets can be negated using the ^ metacharacter. Here's
an example:

Text

```
sales1.xls
orders3.xls
sales2.xls
sales3.xls
apac1.xls
europe2.xls
sam.xls
na1.xls
na2.xls
sa1.xls
ca1.xls
```

RegEx

```
[ns]a[^0-9]\.xls
```

Result

```
sales1.xls
orders3.xls
sales2.xls
sales3.xls
apac1.xls
europe2.xls
sam.xls
na1.xls
na2.xls
sa1.xls
ca1.xls
```

Analysis

The pattern used in this example is the exact opposite of the one used previously. `[0-9]` matches all digits (and only digits). `[^0-9]` matches anything by the specified range of digits. As such, `[ns]a[^0-9]\.xls` matches `sam.xls` but not `na1.xls`, `na2.xls`, or `sa1.xls`.

> **Note**
>
> `^` negates all characters or ranges in a set, not just the character or range that it precedes.

Summary

Metacharacters `[` and `]` are used to define sets of characters, any one of which must match (OR in contrast to AND). Character sets may be enumerated explicitly or specified as ranges using the `-` metacharacter. Character sets may be negated using `^`; this forces a match of anything but the specified characters.

Lesson 4

Using Metacharacters

Metacharacters were introduced in Lesson 2, "Matching Single Characters." In this lesson you'll learn about additional metacharacters used to match specific characters or character types.

Escaping Revisited

Before venturing deeply into the world of metacharacters, it is important to revisit a topic mentioned in passing previously: escaping.

Metacharacters are characters that have special meaning within regular expressions. The period (.) is a metacharacter; it is used to match any single character (as explained in Lesson 2). Similarly, the left bracket ([) is a metacharacter; it is used to mark the beginning of a set (as explained in Lesson 3, "Matching Sets of Characters").

Because metacharacters take on special significance when used in regular expressions, these characters cannot be used to refer to themselves. For example, you cannot use a [to match [or . to match .. Take a look at the following example. A regular expression is being used to attempt to match a JavaScript array containing [and]:

Text

```
var myArray = new Array();
...
if (myArray[0] == 0) {
...
}
```

RegEx

```
myArray[0]
```

Result

```
var myArray = new Array();
...
if (myArray[0] == 0) {
...
}
```

Analysis

In this example, the block of text is a JavaScript code snippet (or a part of one). The regular expression is the type that you would likely use within a text editor. It was supposed to have matched the literal text `myArray[0]`, but it did not. Why not? `[` and `]` are regular expression metacharacters that are used to define a set (but not the characters `[` and `]`). As such, `myArray[0]` would match `myArray` followed by one of the members of the set, and `0` is the only member. Therefore, `myArray[0]` would only ever match `myArray0`.

As explained in Lesson 2, metacharacters can be escaped by preceding them with a backslash. Therefore, `\.` matches `.`, and `\[` matches `[`. Every metacharacter can be escaped by preceding it with a backslash; when escaped, the character itself is matched instead of the special metacharacter meaning. To actually match `[` and `]`, those characters must be escaped. Following is that same example again, this time with the metacharacters escaped:

Text

```
var myArray = new Array();
...
if (myArray[0] == 0) {
...
}
```

RegEx

```
myArray\[0\]
```

Result

```
var myArray = new Array();
...
if (myArray[0] == 0) {
...
}
```

Analysis

This time the search worked. `\[` matches `[` and `\]` matches `]`; so `myArray\[0\]` matches `myArray[0]`.

Using a regular expression in this example is somewhat unnecessary—a simple text match would have sufficed and would have been easier, too. But imagine if you wanted to match not just `myArray[0]` but also `myArray[1]`, `myArray[2]`, and so on. Then using a regular expression would make a lot of sense. You would escape `[` and `]` and specify the characters to match in between them. If you wanted to match array elements `0` through `9`, you might use a regular expression like the following:

```
myArray\[[0-9]\]
```

> **Tip**
>
> Any metacharacter, not just the ones mentioned here, can be escaped by preceding it with a backslash.

> **Caution**
>
> Metacharacters that are part of a pair (such as `[` or `]`) must be escaped if not being used as a metacharacter, or else the regular expression parser may throw an error.

`\` is used to escape metacharacters. This means that `\` is itself a metacharacter; it is used to escape other characters. As noted in Lesson 2, to refer to `\`, you would need to escape the reference as `\\`.

Take a look at the following simple example. The text is a file path using backslashes (used in Windows). Now imagine that you need to use this path on Linux, and as such, you need to locate all backslashes to change them to slashes:

Text

```
\home\ben\sales\
```

RegEx

```
\\
```

Result

\home\ben\sales\

Analysis

`\\` matches `\`, and four matches are found. Had you just specified `\` as the regular expression, you would likely have generated an error (because the regular expression parser would right-fully assume that your expression was incomplete; after all, `\` is always followed by another character in a regular expression).

Matching Whitespace Characters

Metacharacters generally fall into two categories: those used to match text (such as .) and those used as part of regular expression syntax (such as [and]). You'll be discovering many more metacharacters of both types, starting with the whitespace metacharacters.

When you are performing regular expression searches, you'll often need to match nonprinting whitespace characters embedded in your text. For example, you may want to find all tab characters, or you may want to find line breaks. Because typing this character into your regular expressions directly would be very tricky (to say the least), you can use the special metacharacters listed in Table 4.1.

Table 4.1   **Whitespace Metacharacters**

Metacharacter	Description
[\b]	Backspace
\f	Form feed
\n	Line feed
\r	Carriage return
\t	Tab
\v	Vertical tab

Let's look at an example. The following block of text contains a series of records in comma-delimited format (often called CSV). Before processing the records, you need to remove any blank lines in the data. The example follows:

Text

```
"101","Ben","Forta"
"102","Jim","James"

"103","Roberta","Robertson"
"104","Bob","Bobson"
```

RegEx

```
\r\n\r\n
```

Result

```
"101","Ben","Forta"
"102","Jim","James"

"103","Roberta","Robertson"
"104","Bob","Bobson"
```

Analysis

\r\n matches a carriage return line feed combination, used (by Windows) as an end-of-line marker. Searching for \r\n\r\n therefore matches two end-of-line markers, and thus the blank line in between two records.

> **Tip**
>
> I just stated that \r\n is used by Windows as an end-of-line marker. However, Unix (and Linux) as well as Mac OSX systems use just the linefeed character. On those system, you'll probably just want to use \n (and not the \r). The ideal regular expression should probably accommodate both—an optional \r and a required \n. You'll revisit this example in the next lesson.

You'll likely find frequent uses for \r and \n as well as \t (tab). The other whitespace characters tend to be used infrequently.

> **Note**
>
> You've now seen a variation of the metacharacter. The . and [are metacharacters unless they are escaped. f and n, for example, are metacharacters only when they are escaped. Left unescaped, they are literal characters that match only themselves.

Matching Specific Character Types

Thus far, you have seen how to match specific characters, any characters (using .), and one of a set of characters (using [and]), and how to negate matches (using ^). Sets of characters (matching one of a set) is the most common form of matching, and special metacharacters can be used in lieu of commonly used sets. These metacharacters are said to match *classes* of characters. Class metacharacters are never actually needed (you can always enumerate the characters to match or use ranges), but you will undoubtedly find them to be incredibly useful.

> **Note**
>
> The classes listed next are the basics supported in almost all regular expression implementations.

Matching Digits (and Nondigits)

As you learned in Lesson 3, [0-9] is a shortcut for [0123456789] and is used to match any digit. To match anything other than a digit, the set can be negated as [^0-9]. Table 4.2 lists the class shortcuts for digits and nondigits.

Table 4.2 **Digit Metacharacters**

Metacharacter	Description
\d	Any digit (same as [0-9])
\D	Any nondigit (same as [^0-9])

To demonstrate the use of these metacharacters, let's revisit a prior example:

Text

```
var myArray = new Array();
...
if (myArray[0] == 0) {
...
}
```

RegEx

```
myArray\[\d\]
```

Result

```
var myArray = new Array();
...
if (myArray[0] == 0) {
...
}
```

Analysis

\[matches [, \d matches any single digit, and \] matches], so that myArray\[\d\] matches myArray[0]. myArray\[\d\] is shorthand for myArray\[0-9\], which is shorthand for myArray\[0123456789\]. This regular expression would also have matched myArray[1], myArray[2], and so on (but not myArray[10]).

> **Tip**
>
> As you can see, there are almost always multiple ways to define any regular expression. Feel free to pick the syntax that you are most comfortable with.

> **Caution**
>
> Regular expression syntax is case sensitive. \d matches digits. \D is the exact opposite of \d; it only matches nondigits. The same is true of the class metacharacters you'll see next.
>
> This is true even when performing non-case-sensitive matching, in which case the text being matched will not be case sensitive, but special characters (such as \d) will be.

Matching Alphanumeric Characters (and Nonalphanumeric Characters)

Another frequently used set are all the alphanumeric characters, A through Z (in uppercase and lowercase), the digits, and the underscore (often used in file and directory names, application variable names, database object names, and more). Table 4.3 lists the class shortcuts for alphanumeric characters and nonalphanumeric characters.

Table 4.3 **Alphanumeric Metacharacters**

Metacharacter	Description
\w	Any alphanumeric character in upper- or lowercase and underscore (same as `[a-zA-Z0-9_]`)
\W	Any nonalphanumeric or underscore character (same as `[^a-zA-Z0-9_]`)

The following example is an excerpt from a database containing records with U.S. ZIP codes and Canadian postal codes:

Text

```
11213
A1C2E3
48075
48237
M1B4F2
90046
H1H2H2
```

RegEx

```
\w\d\w\d\w\d
```

Result

```
11213
A1C2E3
48075
48237
M1B4F2
90046
H1H2H2
```

Analysis

The pattern used here combines \w and \d metacharacters to retrieve only the Canadian postal codes.

> **Note**
>
> The example here worked properly. But is it correct? Think about it. Why were the U.S. ZIP codes not matched? Is it because they are made up of just digits, or is there some other reason?
>
> I'm not going to give you the answer to this question because, well, the pattern worked. The key here is that there is rarely a right or wrong regular expression (as long as it works, of course). More often than not, there are varying degrees of complexity that correspond to varying degrees of pattern-matching strictness.

Matching Whitespace (and Nonwhitespace)

The final class you should look at is the whitespace class. Earlier in this lesson, you learned the metacharacters for specific whitespace characters. Table 4.4 lists the class shortcuts for all whitespace characters.

Table 4.4 **Whitespace Metacharacters**

Metacharacter	Description
\s	Any whitespace character (same as [\f\n\r\t\v])
\S	Any nonwhitespace character (same as [^\f\n\r\t\v])

> **Note**
>
> [\b], the backspace metacharacter, is not included in \s or excluded by \S.

Specifying Hexadecimal or Octal Values

Although you'll not find yourself needing to refer to specific characters by their octal or hexadecimal value, it is worth noting that this is doable.

Using Hexadecimal Values

Hexadecimal (base 16) values may be specified by preceding them with \x. Therefore, \x0A (ASCII character 10, the linefeed character) is functionally equivalent to \n.

Using Octal Values

Octal (base 8) values may be specified as two- or three-digit numbers proceeded by \0. Therefore, \011 (ASCII character 9, the tab character) is functionally equivalent to \t.

> **Note**
>
> Many regular expression implementations also allow the specification of control characters using `\c`. For example, `\cZ` would match `Ctrl-Z`. In practice, you'll find very little use for this syntax.

Using POSIX Character Classes

A lesson on metacharacters and shortcuts for various character sets would not be complete without a mention of the POSIX character classes. POSIX is a special set of standard character classes, and these are yet another form of shortcut that is supported by many (but not all) regular expression implementations.

> **Note**
>
> JavaScript does not support the use of POSIX character classes in regular expressions.

Table 4.5   **POSIX Character Classes**

Class	Description
`[:alnum:]`	Any letter or digit (same as `[a-zA-Z0-9]`)
`[:alpha:]`	Any letter (same as `[a-zA-Z]`)
`[:blank:]`	Space or tab (same as `[\t]`)
`[:cntrl:]`	ASCII control characters (ASCII 0 through 31 and 127)
`[:digit:]`	Any digit (same as `[0-9]`)
`[:graph:]`	Same as `[:print:]` but excludes space
`[:lower:]`	Any lowercase letter (same as `[a-z]`)
`[:print:]`	Any printable character
`[:punct:]`	Any character that is in neither `[:alnum:]` nor `[:cntrl:]`
`[:space:]`	Any whitespace character including spaces (same as `[\f\n\r\t\v]`)
`[:upper:]`	Any uppercase letter (same as `[A-Z]`)
`[:xdigit:]`	Any hexadecimal digit (same as `[a-fA-F0-9]`)

The POSIX syntax is quite different from the metacharacters seen thus far. To demonstrate the use of POSIX classes, let's revisit an example from Lesson 3. The example used a regular expression to locate RGB values in a block of HTML code:

Text

```
body {
    background-color: #fefbd8;
}
h1 {
    background-color: #0000ff;
}
div {
    background-color: #d0f4e6;
}
span {
    background-color: #f08970;
}
```

RegEx

```
#[[:xdigit:]][[:xdigit:]][[:xdigit:]][[:xdigit:]][[:xdigit:]][[:xdigit:]]
```

Result

```
body {
    background-color: #fefbd8;
}
h1 {
    background-color: #0000ff;
}
div {
    background-color: #d0f4e6;
}
span {
    background-color: #f08970;
}
```

Analysis

The pattern used in the previous lesson repeated the character set [0-9A-Fa-f] six times. Here each [0-9A-Fa-f] has been replaced by [[:xdigit:]]. The result is the same.

Note

Notice that the regular expression used here starts with `[[` and ends with `]]` (two sets of brackets). This is important and required when using POSIX classes. POSIX classes are enclosed within `[:` and `:]`; the POSIX we used is `[:xdigit:]` (not `:xdigit:`). The outer `[` and `]` are defining the set; the inner `[` and `]` are part of the POSIX class itself.

Caution

All 12 POSIX classes enumerated here are generally supported in any implementation that supports POSIX. However, there may be subtle variances from the preceding descriptions.

Summary

Building on the basics of character and set matching shown in Lessons 2 and 3, this lesson introduced metacharacters that match specific characters (such as tab or linefeed) or entire sets or classes of characters (such as digits or alphanumeric characters). These shortcut metacharacters and POSIX classes may be used to simplify regular expression patterns.

Lesson 5
Repeating Matches

In the previous lessons, you learned how to match individual characters using a variety of metacharacters and special class sets. In this lesson, you'll learn how to match multiple repeating characters or sets of characters.

How Many Matches?

You've learned all the basics of regular expression pattern matching, but all the examples have had one very serious limitation. Consider what it would take to write a regular expression to match an email address. The basic format of an email address looks something like the following:

```
text@text.text
```

Using the metacharacters discussed in the previous lesson, you could create a regular expression like the following:

```
\w@\w\.\w
```

The `\w` would match all alphanumeric characters (plus an underscore, which is valid in an email address); @ does not need to be escaped, but . does.

This is a perfectly legal regular expression, albeit a rather useless one. It would match an email address that looked like a@b.c (which, although syntactically legal, is obviously not a valid address). The problem with it is that `\w` matches a single character and you can't know how many characters to test for. After all, the following are all valid email addresses, but they all have a different number of characters before the @:

```
b@forta.com
ben@forta.com
bforta@forta.com
```

What you need is a way to match multiple characters, and this is doable using one of several special metacharacters.

Matching One or More Characters

To match one or more instances of a character (or set), simply append a + character. + matches one or more characters (at least one; zero would not match). Whereas a matches a, a+ matches one or more as. Similarly, whereas [0-9] matches any digits, [0-9]+ matches one or more consecutive digits.

> ### Tip
>
> When you use + with sets, the + should be placed outside the set. Therefore, [0-9]+ is correct, but [0-9+] is not.
>
> [0-9+] actually is a valid regular expression, but it will not match one or more digits. Rather, it defines a set of 0 through 9 or the + character, and any single digit or plus sign will match. Although legal, it is probably not what you'd want.

Let's revisit the email address example, this time using + to match one or more characters:

Text

```
Send personal email to ben@forta.com. For questions
about a book use support@forta.com. Feel free to send
unsolicited email to spam@forta.com (wouldn't it be
nice if it were that simple, huh?).
```

RegEx

```
\w+@\w+\.\w+
```

Result

```
Send personal email to ben@forta.com. For questions
about a book use support@forta.com. Feel free to send
unsolicited email to spam@forta.com (wouldn't it be
nice if it were that simple, huh?).
```

Analysis

The pattern matched all three addresses correctly. The regular expression first matches one or more alphanumeric characters using \w+. Next it matches @ followed by one or more characters, again using \w+. It then matches . (using the escaped \.) and another \w+ to match the end of the address.

> ### Tip
>
> + is a metacharacter. To match a + you'll need to escape it as \+.

+ can also be used to match one or more sets of characters. To demonstrate this, the following example shows the same regular expression but with slightly different text:

Text

```
Send personal email to ben@forta.com or
ben.forta@forta.com. For questions about a
book use support@forta.com. If your message
is urgent try ben@urgent.forta.com. Feel
free to send unsolicited email to
spam@forta.com (wouldn't it be nice if
it were that simple, huh?).
```

RegEx

```
\w+@\w+\.\w+
```

Result

```
Send personal email to ben@forta.com or
ben.forta@forta.com. For questions about a
book use support@forta.com. If your message
is urgent try ben@urgent.forta.com. Feel
free to send unsolicited email to
spam@forta.com (wouldn't it be nice if
it were that simple, huh?).
```

Analysis

The regular expression matched five addresses, but two of them are incomplete. Why is this? `\w+@\w+\.\w+` makes no accommodations for `.` characters before the `@`, and it allows only a single `.` separating the two strings after the `@`. Although ben.forta@forta.com is a perfectly legal email address, the regular expression matched only forta (instead of ben.forta) because `\w` matches alphanumeric characters but not a `.` in the middle of a string of text.

What we need here is to match either `\w` or `.`, or in regular expression parlance, a set of `[\w\.]`. Following is a revised example:

Text

```
Send personal email to ben@forta.com or
ben.forta@forta.com. For questions about a
book use support@forta.com. If your message
is urgent try ben@urgent.forta.com. Feel
free to send unsolicited email to
spam@forta.com (wouldn't it be nice if
it were that simple, huh?).
```

RegEx

```
[\w.]+@[\w.]+\.\w+
```

Result

Send personal email to `ben@forta.com` or
`ben.forta@forta.com`. For questions about a
book use `support@forta.com`. If your message
is urgent try `ben@urgent.forta.com`. Feel
free to send unsolicited email to
`spam@forta.com` (wouldn't it be nice if
it were that simple, huh?).

Analysis

That seemed to do the trick. `[\w.]+` matches one or more instances of any alphanumeric character, underscore, and `.`, and so `ben.forta` is matched. `[\w.]+` is also used for the string after the `@` so that deeper domain (or host) names are matched.

> **Note**
>
> Notice that for the final match, you used `\w+` and not `[\w.]+`. Can you figure out why? Try using `[\w.]` for the final pattern and see what is wrong with the second, third, and fourth matches.

> **Note**
>
> You'll notice that the `.` in the set was not escaped, and it matched `.` anyway (it was treated as a literal as opposed to a metacharacter). Generally, metacharacters such as `.` and `+` are considered to be literal text when used within sets, and therefore they need not be escaped. However, escaping them does no harm. `[\w.]` is functionally equivalent to `[\w\.]`.

Matching Zero or More Characters

`+` matches one or more characters. Zero characters will not match—there has to be at least one. But what if you wanted to match entirely optional characters so that zero characters would be allowed?

To do this, you use the `*` metacharacter. `*` is used exactly like `+`; it is placed right after a character or a set and will match zero or more instances of the character or set. Therefore, pattern `B.* Forta` would match `B Forta`, `B. Forta`, `Ben Forta`, and other combinations, too.

To demonstrate the use of `+`, take a look at a modified version of the email example:

Text

```
Hello .ben@forta.com is my email address.
```

RegEx

```
[\w.]+@[\w.]+\.\w+
```

Result

Hello `.ben@forta.com` is my email address.

Analysis

You will recall that `[\w.]+` matches one or more instances of alphanumeric characters and `.`, and so `.ben` matched. There is obviously a typo in the preceding text (an extraneous period in the middle of the text), but that is irrelevant. The bigger issue is that although `.` is a valid character in an email address, it is not a valid character with which to start an email address.

In other words, what you really need to match is alphanumeric text with optional additional characters, like this:

Text

```
Hello .ben@forta.com is my email address.
```

RegEx

```
\w+[\w.]*@[\w.]+\.\w+
```

Result

Hello `.ben@forta.com` is my email address.

Analysis

This pattern is looking increasingly complex (RegEx patterns often looks far more complex than they actually are), so let's look at it together. `\w+` matches any alphanumeric character but not `.` (the valid characters with which to start an email address). After the initial valid characters, it is indeed possible to have a `.` and additional characters, although these may in fact not be present. `[\w.]*` matches zero or more instances of `.` or alphanumeric characters, which is exactly what was needed.

> **Note**
>
> Think of `*` as being the *make it optional* metacharacter. Unlike `+`, which requires at least one match, `*` matches any number of matches if present, but does not require that any be present.

> **Tip**
>
> `*` is a metacharacter. To match an `*` you'll need to escape it as `\*`.

Matching Zero or One Characters

One other very useful metacharacter is `?`. Like `+`, `?` matches optional text (and so zero instances will match). But unlike `+`, `?` matches only zero or one instance of a character (or set), but not more than one. As such, `?` is very useful for matching specific, single optional characters in a block of text.

Consider the following example:

Text

```
The URL is http://www.forta.com/, to connect
securely use https://www.forta.com/ instead.
```

RegEx

```
http:\/\/[\w.\/]+
```

Result

```
The URL is http://www.forta.com/, to connect
securely use https://www.forta.com/ instead.
```

Analysis

The pattern used to match a URL is `http:\/\/` (which is literal text, including two escaped slashes, and therefore matches only itself) followed by `[\w./]+`, which matches one or more instances of a set that allows alphanumeric characters, `.`, and forward slash. This pattern can match only the first URL (the one that starts with `http://`) but not the second (the one that starts with `https://`). And `s*` (zero or more instances of `s`) would not be correct because that would then also allow `httpsssss://` (which is definitely not valid).

The solution? To use `s?` as seen in the following example:

Text

```
The URL is http://www.forta.com/, to connect
securely use https://www.forta.com/ instead.
```

RegEx

```
https?:\/\/[\w.\/]+
```

Result

```
The URL is http://www.forta.com/, to connect
securely use https://www.forta.com/ instead.
```

Analysis

The pattern here begins with `https?://`. `?` means that the preceding character (the `s`) should be matched if it is not present, or if a single instance of it is present. In other words, `https?://` matches both `http://` and `https://` (but nothing else).

Incidentally, using `?` is the solution to a problem alluded to in the previous lesson. You looked at an example where `\r\n` was being used to match an end-of-line marker, and I mentioned that on Unix or Linux boxes, you would need to use `\n` (without the `\r`) and that an ideal solution would be to match an optional `\r` followed by a `\n`. That example follows again, this time using a slightly modified regular expression:

Text

```
"101","Ben","Forta"
"102","Jim","James"

"103","Roberta","Robertson"
"104","Bob","Bobson"
```

RegEx

```
[\r]?\n[\r]?\n
```

Result

```
"101","Ben","Forta"
"102","Jim","James"

"103","Roberta","Robertson"
"104","Bob","Bobson"
```

Analysis

`[\r]?\n` matches an optional single instance of `\r` followed by a required `\n`.

Tip

You'll notice that the regular expression here used `[\r]?` instead of `\r?`. `[\r]` defines a set containing a single metacharacter, a set of one, so `[\r]?` is actually functionally identical to `\r?`. `[]` is usually used to define a set of characters, but some developers like to use it even around single characters to prevent ambiguity (to make it stand out so that you know exactly what the following metacharacter applies to). If you are using both `[]` and `?`, make sure to place the `?` outside of the set. Therefore, `http[s]?://` is correct, but `http[s?]://` is not.

Tip

`?` is a metacharacter. To match an `?` you'll need to escape it as `\?`.

Using Intervals

+, *, and ? are used to solve many problems with regular expressions, but sometimes they are not enough. Consider the following:

- + and * match an unlimited number of characters. They provide no way to set a maximum number of characters to match.

- The only minimums supported by +, *, and ? are zero or one. They provide no way to set an explicit minimum number of matches.

- There is also no way to specify an exact number of matches desired.

To solve these problems, and to provide a greater degree of control over repeating matches, regular expressions allow for the use of *intervals*. Intervals are specified between the { and } characters.

> **Note**
>
> { and } are metacharacters and, as such, should be escaped using \ when needed as literal text. It is worth noting that many regular expression implementations seem to be able to correctly process { and } even if they are not escaped (being able to determine when they are literal and when they are metacharacters). However, it is best not to rely on this behavior and to escape the characters when needing them as literals.

Exact Interval Matching

To specify an exact number of matches, you place that number between { and }. Therefore, {3} means match three instances of the previous character or set. If there are only two instances, the pattern would not match.

To demonstrate this, let's revisit the RGB example (used in Lessons 3 and 4). You will recall that RGB values are specified as three sets of hexadecimal numbers (each of two characters). The first pattern used to match an RGB value was the following:

`#[0-9A-Fa-f][0-9A-Fa-f][0-9A-Fa-f][0-9A-Fa-f][0-9A-Fa-f][0-9A-Fa-f]`

In Lesson 4, you used a POSIX class and changed the pattern to

`#[[:xdigit:]][[:xdigit:]][[:xdigit:]][[:xdigit:]][[:xdigit:]][[:xdigit:]]`

The problem with both patterns is that you had to repeat the exact character set (or class) six times. Here is the same example, this time using interval matching:

Text

```
body {
    background-color: #fefbd8;
}
h1 {
    background-color: #0000ff;
}
div {
    background-color: #d0f4e6;
}
span {
    background-color: #f08970;
}
```

RegEx

```
#[A-Fa-f0-9]{6}
```

Result

```
body {
    background-color: #fefbd8;
}
h1 {
    background-color: #0000ff;
}
div {
    background-color: #d0f4e6;
}
span {
    background-color: #f08970;
}
```

Analysis

`[A-Fa-f0-9]` matches a single hexadecimal character, and `{6}` repeats that match six times. This would have worked just as well using POSIX.

Range Interval Matching

Intervals may also be used to specify a range of values—a minimum and a maximum number of instances that are to be matched. Ranges are specified as `{2,4}` (which would mean a minimum of 2 and a maximum of 4). An example of this is a regular expression used to validate the format of dates:

Text

```
4/8/17
10-6-2018
2/2/2
01-01-01
```

RegEx

```
\d{1,2}[-\/]\d{1,2}[-\/]\d{2,4}
```

Result

```
4/8/17
10-6-2018
2/2/2
01-01-01
```

Analysis

The dates listed here are values that users may have entered into a form field—values that must be validated as correctly formatted dates. `\d{1,2}` matches one or two digits (this test is used for both day and month); `\d{2,4}` matches the year; and `[-\/]` matches either – or / as the date separator. As such, three dates were matched, but not `2/2/2` (which fails because the year is too short).

> **Tip**
>
> The regular expression used here escapes / as \/. In many regular expression implementations this is unnecessary, but some regular expression parsers do require this. As such, it is a good idea to always escape /.

It is important to note that the preceding pattern does not validate dates; invalid dates such as `54/67/9999` would pass the test. All it does is validate the format (the step usually taken before checking the validity of the dates themselves).

> **Note**
>
> Intervals may begin with 0. Interval `{0,3}` means match zero, one, two, or three instances.
>
> As seen previously, ? matches zero or one instance of whatever precedes it. As such, ? is functionally equivalent to `{0,1}`.

"At Least" Interval Matching

The final use of intervals is to specify the minimum number of instances to be matched (without any maximum). The syntax for this type of interval is similar to that of a range, but with the maximum omitted. For example, $\{3,\}$ means match at least three instances, or stated differently, match three or more instances.

Let's look at an example which combines much of what was covered in this lesson. In this example, a regular expression is used to locate all orders valued at $100 or more:

Text

```
1001: $496.80
1002: $1290.69
1003: $26.43
1004: $613.42
1005: $7.61
1006: $414.90
1007: $25.00
```

RegEx

```
\d+: \$\d{3,}\.\d{2}
```

Result

```
1001: $496.80
1002: $1290.69
1003: $26.43
1004: $613.42
1005: $7.61
1006: $414.90
1007: $25.00
```

Analysis

The preceding text is a report showing order numbers followed by the order value. The regular expression first uses `\d+:` to match the order number (this could have been omitted, in which case the price would have matched and not the entire line including the order number). The pattern `\$\d{3,}\.\d{2}` is used to match the price itself. `\$` matches $, `\d{3,}` matches numbers of at least three digits (and thus at least $100), `\.` matches ., and finally `\d{2}` matches the two digits after the decimal point. The pattern correctly matches four of the seven orders.

Tip

Be careful when using this form of interval. If you omit the , the test will change from matching a minimum number of instances to matching an exact number of instances.

Note

+ is functionally equivalent to $\{1,\}$.

Preventing Over Matching

? matches are limited in scope (zero or one matches only), and so are interval matches when using exact amounts or ranges. But the other forms of repetition described in this lesson can match an unlimited number of matches—sometimes too many.

All the examples thus far were carefully chosen so as not to run into over matching, but consider this next example. The text that follows is part of a Web page and contains text with embedded HTML <b> tags. The regular expression needs to match any text within <b> tags (perhaps so as to be able to replace the formatting). Here's the example:

Text

```
This offer is not available to customers
living in <b>AK</b> and <b>HI</b>.
```

RegEx

```
<[Bb]>.*<\/[Bb]>
```

Result

```
This offer is not available to customers
living in <b>AK</b> and <b>HI</b>.
```

Analysis

< [Bb] > matches the opening <b> tag (in either uppercase or lowercase), and </ [Bb] > matches the closing </b> tag (also in either uppercase or lowercase). But instead of two matches, only one was found; the . * matched everything after the first <b> until the last </b> so that the text AK</b> and <b>HI was matched. This includes the text we wanted matched, but also other instances of the tags as well.

The reason for this is that metacharacters like * and + are *greedy*; that is, they look for the greatest possible match as opposed to the smallest. It is almost as if the matching starts from the end of the text, working backward until the next match is found, in contrast to starting from the beginning. This is deliberate and by design, quantifiers are greedy.

But what if you don't want greedy matching? The solution is to use *lazy* versions of these quantifiers (they are referred to as being *lazy* because they match the fewest characters instead of the most). Lazy quantifiers are defined by appending an ? to the quantifier being used, and each of the greedy quantifiers has a lazy equivalent as listed in Table 5.1.

Table 5.1   **Greedy and Lazy Quantifiers**

Greedy	Lazy
`*`	`*?`
`+`	`+?`
`{n,}`	`{n,}?`

`*?` is the lazy version of `*`, so let's revisit our example, this time using `*?`:

Text

```
This offer is not available to customers
living in <b>AK</b> and <b>HI</b>.
```

RegEx

```
<[Bb]>.*?<\/[Bb]>
```

Result

```
This offer is not available to customers
living in <b>AK</b> and <b>HI</b>.
```

Analysis

That worked. By using the lazy `*?` only AK, was matched in the first match, allowing HI to be matched independently.

> **Note**
>
> Most of the examples in this book use greedy quantifiers so as to keep patterns as simple as possible. However, feel free to replace these with lazy quantifiers when needed.

Summary

The real power of regular expression patterns becomes apparent when working with repeating matches. This lesson introduced + (match one or more), * (match zero or more), and ? (match zero or one) as ways to perform repeating matches. For greater control, intervals may be used to specify the exact number of repetitions as well as minimums and maximums. Quantifiers are greedy and may over match; to prevent this from occurring, use lazy quantifiers.

Lesson 6
Position Matching

You've now learned how to match all sorts of characters in all sorts of combinations and repetitions and in any location within text. However, it is sometimes necessary to match at specific locations within a block of text, and this requires position matching, which is explained in this lesson.

Using Boundaries

Position matching is used to specify where within a string of text a match should occur. To understand the need for position matching, consider the following example:

Text

```
The cat scattered his food all over the room.
```

RegEx

```
cat
```

Result

```
The cat scattered his food all over the room.
```

Analysis

The pattern cat matches all occurrences of cat, even cat within the word scattered. This may, in fact, be the desired outcome, but more than likely it is not. If you were performing the search to replace all occurrences of cat with dog, you would end up with the following nonsense:

```
The dog sdogtered his food all over the room.
```

That brings us to the use of *boundaries*, or special metacharacters used to specify the position (or boundary) before or after a pattern.

Using Word Boundaries

The first boundary (and one of the most commonly used) is the word boundary specified as \b. As its name suggests, \b is used to match the start or end of a word.

To demonstrate the use of \b, here is the previous example again, this time with the boundaries specified:

Text

```
The cat scattered his food all over the room.
```

RegEx

```
\bcat\b
```

Result

```
The cat scattered his food all over the room.
```

Analysis

The word cat has a space before and after it, and so it matches \bcat\b (space is one of the characters used to separate words). The word cat in scattered, however, did not match, because the character before it is s and the character after it is t (neither of which match \b).

> **Note**
>
> So what exactly is it that \b matches? Regular expression engines do not understand English, or any language for that matter, and so they don't know what word boundaries are. \b simply matches a location between characters that are usually parts of words (alphanumeric characters and underscore, text that would be matched by \w) and anything else (text that would be matched by \W).

It is important to realize that to match a whole word, \b must be used both before and after the text to be matched. Consider this example:

Text

```
The captain wore his cap and cape proudly as
he sat listening to the recap of how his
crew saved the men from a capsized vessel.
```

RegEx

```
\bcap
```

Result

The captain wore his cap and cape proudly as
he sat listening to the recap of how his
crew saved the men from a capsized vessel.

Analysis

The pattern \bcap matches any word that starts with cap, and so four words matched, including three that are not the word cap.

Following is the same example but with only a trailing \b:

Text

```
The captain wore his cap and cape proudly as
he sat listening to the recap of how his
crew saved the men from a capsized vessel.
```

RegEx

```
cat\b
```

Result

The captain wore his cap and cape proudly as
he sat listening to the recap of how his
crew saved the men from a capsized vessel.

Analysis

cap\b matches any word that ends with cap, and so two matches were found, including one that is not the word cap.

If only the word cap was to be matched, the correct pattern to use would be \bcap\b.

> **Note**
>
> \b does not actually match a character; rather, it matches a position. So the string matched using \bcat\b will be three characters in length (c, a, and t), not five characters in length.

To specifically not match at a word boundary, use \B. This example uses \B metacharacters to help locate hyphens with extraneous spaces around them:

Text

```
Please enter the nine-digit id as it
appears on your color - coded pass-key.
```

RegEx

```
\B-\B
```

Result

```
Please enter the nine-digit id as it
appears on your color █ coded pass-key.
```

Analysis

`\B-\B` matches a hyphen that is surrounded by word-break characters. The hyphens in `nine-digit` and `pass-key` do not match, but the one in `color - coded` does.

> **Note**
>
> As seen in Lesson 4, "Using Metacharacters," uppercase metacharacters usually negate the functionality of their lowercase equivalents.

> **Note**
>
> Some regular expression implementations support two additional metacharacters. Whereas `\b` matches the start or end of a word, `\<` matches only the start of a word and `\>` matches only the end of a word. Although the use of these characters provides additional control, support for them is very limited (they are supported in `egrep`, but not in many other implementations).

Defining String Boundaries

Word boundaries are used to locate matches based on word position (start of word, end of word, entire word, and so on). String boundaries perform a similar function but are used to match patterns at the start or end of an entire string. The string boundary metacharacters are `^` for start of string and `$` for end of string.

> **Note**
>
> In Lesson 3, "Matching Sets of Characters," you learned that `^` is used to negate a set. How can it also be used to indicate the start of a string?
>
> `^` is one of several metacharacters that has multiple uses. It negates a set only if in a set (enclosed within `[` and `]`) and is the first character after the opening `]`. Outside of a set, and at the beginning of a pattern, `^` matches the start of a string.

To demonstrate the use of string boundaries, look at the following example. Valid XML documents begin with `<?xml>` and likely have additional attributes (possibly a version number, as in `<xml version="1.0" ?>`). Following is a simple test to check whether text is an XML document:

Text

```
<?xml version="1.0" encoding="UTF-8" ?>
<wsdl:definitions targetNamespace="http://tips.cf"
xmlns:impl="http://tips.cf" xmlns:intf="http://tips.cf"
xmlns:apachesoap="http://xml.apache.org/xml-soap"
```

RegEx

```
<\?xml.*\?>
```

Result

```
<?xml version="1.0" encoding="UTF-8" ?>
<wsdl:definitions targetNamespace="http://tips.cf"
xmlns:impl="http://tips.cf" xmlns:intf="http://tips.cf"
xmlns:apachesoap="http://xml.apache.org/xml-soap"
```

Analysis

The pattern appeared to work. `<\?xml` matches `<?xml`, `.*` matches any other text (zero or more instances of `.`), and `\?>` matches the end `?>`.

But this is a very inaccurate test. Look at the example that follows; the same pattern is being used to match text with extraneous text before the XML opening:

Text

```
This is bad, real bad!
<?xml version="1.0" encoding="UTF-8" ?>
<wsdl:definitions targetNamespace="http://tips.cf"
xmlns:impl="http://tips.cf" xmlns:intf="http://tips.cf"
xmlns:apachesoap="http://xml.apache.org/xml-soap"
```

RegEx

```
<\?xml.*\?>
```

Result

```
This is bad, real bad!
<?xml version="1.0" encoding="UTF-8" ?>
<wsdl:definitions targetNamespace="http://tips.cf"
xmlns:impl="http://tips.cf" xmlns:intf="http://tips.cf"
xmlns:apachesoap="http://xml.apache.org/xml-soap"
```

Analysis

The pattern `<\?xml.*\?>` matched the second line of the text. And although the opening XML tag may, in fact, be on the second line of text, this example is definitely invalid (and processing the text as XML could cause all sorts of problems).

What is needed is a test that ensures that the opening XML tag is the first actual text in the string, and that's a perfect job for the `^` metacharacter as seen next:

Text

```
<?xml version="1.0" encoding="UTF-8" ?>
<wsdl:definitions targetNamespace="http://tips.cf"
xmlns:impl="http://tips.cf" xmlns:intf="http://tips.cf"
xmlns:apachesoap="http://xml.apache.org/xml-soap"
```

RegEx

```
^\s*<\?xml.*\?>
```

Result

```
<?xml version="1.0" encoding="UTF-8" ?>
<wsdl:definitions targetNamespace="http://tips.cf"
xmlns:impl="http://tips.cf" xmlns:intf="http://tips.cf"
xmlns:apachesoap="http://xml.apache.org/xml-soap"
```

Analysis

The opening `^` matches the start of string; `^\s*` therefore matches the start of string followed by zero or more whitespace characters (thus handling legitimate spaces, tabs, or line breaks before the XML opening). The complete `^\s*<\?xml.*\?>` thus matches an opening XML tag with any attributes and correctly handles whitespace, too.

> **Tip**
>
> The pattern `^\s*<\?xml.*\?>` worked, but only because the XML shown in this example is incomplete. Had a complete XML listing have been used, you would have seen an example of a greedy quantifier at work. This is, therefore, a great example of when to use `.*?` instead of just `.*`.

`$` is used much the same way. This pattern could be used to check that nothing comes after the closing `</html>` tag in a Web page:

RegEx

```
</[Hh][Tt][Mm][Ll]>\s*$
```

Analysis

Sets are used for each of the characters H, T, M, and L (so as to be able to handle any combination of upper- or lowercase characters), and \s*$ matches any whitespace followed by the end of string.

> **Note**
>
> The pattern ^.*$ is a syntactically correct regular expression; it will almost always find a match, and it is utterly useless. Can you work out what it matches and when it will not find a match?

Using Multiline Mode

^ matches the start of a string and $ matches the end of a string—usually. There is an exception, or rather, a way to change this behavior.

Many regular expression implementations support the use of special metacharacters that modify the behavior of other metacharacters, and one of these is (?m), which enables multiline mode. Multiline mode forces the regular expression engine to treat line breaks as a string separator, so that ^ matches the start of a string or the start after a line break (a new line), and $ matches the end of a string or the end after a line break.

If used, (?m) must be placed at the very front of the pattern, as shown in the following example, which uses a regular expression to locate all JavaScript comments within a block of code:

Text

```
<script>
function doSpellCheck(form, field) {
   // Make sure not empty
   if (field.value == '') {
      return false;
   }
   // Init
   var windowName='spellWindow';
   var spellCheckURL='spell.cfm?formname=comment&fieldname='+field.name;
...
   // Done
   return false;
}
</script>
```

RegEx

```
(?m)^\s*\/\/.*$
```

Result

```
<script>
function doSpellCheck(form, field) {
    // Make sure not empty
    if (field.value == '') {
        return false;
    }
    // Init
    var windowName='spellWindow';
    var spellCheckURL='spell.cfm?formname=comment&fieldname='+field.name;
...
    // Done
    return false;
}
</script>
```

Analysis

`^\s` matches the start of a string, followed by any whitespace, followed by `\/\/` (used to define JavaScript comments), followed by any text, and then an end of string. But that pattern would match only the first comment (and only if it were the only text in the page). The `(?m)` modifier in `(?m)^\s*\/\/.*$` forces the pattern to treat line breaks as string separators, and so all comments were matched.

> **Caution**
>
> `(?m)` is not supported by many regular expression implementations, including JavaScript.

> **Note**
>
> Some regular expression implementations also support the use of `\A` to mark the start of a string and `\Z` to mark the end of a string. If supported, these metacharacters function much like `^` and `$`, respectively, but unlike `^` and `$`, they are not modified by `(?m)` and will therefore not operate in multiline mode.

Summary

Regular expressions can match any blocks of text or text at specific locations within a string. `\b` is used to specify a word boundary (and `\B` does the exact opposite). `^` and `$` mark string boundaries (start of string and end of string, respectively), although when used with the `(?m)` modifier, `^` and `$` will also match strings that start or end at a line break.

Lesson 7

Using Subexpressions

Metacharacters and character matching provide the basic power behind regular expressions, as has been demonstrated in the lessons thus far. In this lesson you'll learn how to group expressions together using subexpressions.

Understanding Subexpressions

Matching multiple occurrences of a character was introduced in Lesson 5, "Repeating Matches." As discussed in that lesson, `\d+` matches one or more digits, and `https?://` matches `http://` or `https://`.

In both of these examples (and indeed, in all the examples thus far) the repetition metacharacters (`?` or `*` or `{2}`, for example) apply to the previous character or metacharacter.

For example, HTML developers often place nonbreaking spaces (using ` `) between words to ensure that text does not wrap between those words. Suppose you needed to locate all repeating HTML nonbreaking spaces (to replace them with something else). Here's the example:

Text

```
Hello, my name is Ben Forta, and I am
the author of multiple books on SQL (including
MySQL, Oracle PL/SQL, and SQL Server T-SQL),
Regular  Expressions, and other subjects.
```

RegEx

```
 {2,}
```

Result

```
Hello, my name is Ben Forta, and I am
the author of multiple books on SQL (including
MySQL, Oracle PL/SQL, and SQL Server T-SQL),
Regular  Expressions, and other subjects.
```

Analysis

  is the entity reference for the HTML nonbreaking spaces. Pattern {2,} should have matched two or more instances of . But it didn't. Why not? Because the {2,} is specifying the number of repetitions of whatever is directly preceding it, in this case a semicolon. ;;;; would have matched, but   will not.

Grouping with Subexpressions

Which brings us to the topic of subexpressions. Subexpressions are parts of a bigger expression; the parts are grouped together so that they are treated as a single entity. Subexpressions are enclosed between (and) characters.

> **Tip**
>
> (and) are metacharacters. To match the actual characters (and), you must escape them as \(and \), respectively.

To demonstrate the use of subexpressions, let's revisit the previous example:

Text

```
Hello, my name is Ben Forta, and I am
the author of multiple books on SQL (including
MySQL, Oracle PL/SQL, and SQL Server T-SQL),
Regular  Expressions, and other subjects.
```

RegEx

```
( ){2,}
```

Result

```
Hello, my name is Ben Forta, and I am
the author of multiple books on SQL (including
MySQL, Oracle PL/SQL, and SQL Server T-SQL),
Regular  Expressions, and other subjects.
```

Analysis

( ) is a subexpression and is treated as a single entity. As such, the {2,} that follows it applies to the entire subexpression (not just the semicolon). That did the trick.

Here is another example—this time a regular expression is used to locate IP addresses. IP addresses are formatted as four sets of numbers separated by periods, such as 12.159.46.200.

Because each of the numbers can be one, two, or three digits, the pattern to match each number could be expressed as \d{1,3}. This is shown in the following example:

Text

```
Pinging hog.forta.com [12.159.46.200]
with 32 bytes of data:
```

RegEx

```
\d{1,3}\.\d{1,3}\.\d{1,3}\.\d{1,3}
```

Result

```
Pinging hog.forta.com [12.159.46.200]
with 32 bytes of data:
```

Analysis

Each instance of \d{1,3} matches one of the numbers in an IP address. The four numbers are separated by ., which is escaped as \.

The pattern \d{1,3}\. (up to 3 digits followed by .) is repeated three times and can thus be expressed as a repetition as well. Following is an alternative version of the same example:

Text

```
Pinging hog.forta.com [12.159.46.200]
with 32 bytes of data:
```

RegEx

```
(\d{1,3}\.){3}\d{1,3}
```

Result

```
Pinging hog.forta.com [12.159.46.200]
with 32 bytes of data:
```

Analysis

This pattern worked just as well as the previous one, but the syntax is different. The expression \d{1,3}\. has been enclosed within (and) to make it a subexpression. (\d{1,3}\.){3} repeats the subexpression three times (for the first three numbers in the IP address), and then \d{1,3} matches the final number.

> **Note**
>
> (\d{1,3}\.){4} is not a viable alternative to the pattern just used. Can you work out why it would have failed in this example?

Tip

Some users like to enclose parts of expressions as subexpressions to improve readability; the previous pattern would be expressed as `(\d{1,3}\.){3}(\d{1,3})`. This practice is perfectly legal, and using it has no effect on the actual behavior of the expression (although there may be performance implications, depending on the regular expression implementation being used).

The use of subexpressions for grouping is so important that it is worthwhile to look at one more example—one not involving repetitions at all. This example attempts to match a year in a user record:

Text

```
ID: 042
SEX: M
DOB: 1967-08-17
Status: Active
```

RegEx

```
19|20\d{2}
```

Result

```
ID: 042
SEX: M
DOB: 1967-08-17
Status: Active
```

Analysis

In this example, the pattern was to have located a four-digit year, but for greater accuracy, the first two digits are explicitly listed as 19 and 20. | is the OR operator, and so 19|20 matches either 19 or 20, and pattern 19|20\d2 should therefore match any four-digit number beginning with 19 or 20 (19 or 20 followed by two digits). Obviously, this did not work. Why not? The | operator looks at what is to its left and to its right and reads pattern 19|20\d{2} as either 19 or 20\d{2} (thinking that the \d{2} is part of the expression that started with 20). In other words, it will match the number 19 or any four-digit year beginning with 20. As such, 19 matched.

The solution is to group 19|20 as a subexpression, as follows:

Text

```
ID: 042
SEX: M
DOB: 1967-08-17
Status: Active
```

RegEx

`(19|20)\d{2}`

Result

```
ID: 042
SEX: M
DOB: 1967-08-17
Status: Active
```

Analysis

With the options all within a subexpression, | knows that what is wanted is one of the options within the group. `(19|20)\d{2}` thus correctly matches `1967` and would also match any four digits beginning with `19` or `20`. At some later date (close to a hundred years from now), if the code needed to be modified to also match years starting with `21`, the pattern could be changed to `(19|20|21)\d{2}`.

> **Note**
>
> Although this lesson covers the use of subexpressions for grouping, there is another extremely important use for subexpressions. This is covered in Lesson 8, "Using Backreferences."

Nesting Subexpressions

Subexpressions may be nested. In fact, subexpressions may be nested within subexpressions nested within subexpressions—you get the picture.

The capability to nest subexpressions allows for incredibly powerful expressions, but it can also make patterns look convoluted, hard to read and decode, and somewhat intimidating. The truth, however, is that nested subexpressions are seldom as complicated as they look.

To demonstrate the use of nested subexpressions, we'll look at the IP address example again. This is the pattern used previously (a subexpression repeated three times followed by the final number):

RegEx

`(\d{1,3}\.){3}\d{1,3}`

So what is wrong with this pattern? Syntactically, nothing. An IP address is indeed made up of four numbers; each is one to three digits and separated by periods. The pattern is correct, and it will match any valid IP address. But that is not all it will match; invalid IP addresses will be matched, too.

An IP address is made up of 4 bytes, and the IP address presented as `12.159.46.200` is a representation of those 4 bytes. The four numbers in an IP address therefore have the range of values in a single byte, `0` to `255`. This means that none of the numbers in an IP address may be greater than `255`. Yet the pattern used will also match `345` and `700` and `999`, all invalid numbers within an IP address.

> **Note**
>
> There is an important lesson here. It is easy to write regular expressions to match what you want and expect. It is much harder to write regular expressions that anticipate all possible scenarios so that they do not match what you do not want to match.

It would be nice to be able to specify a range of valid values, but regular expressions match characters and have no real knowledge of what those characters are. Mathematical calculations are therefore not an option.

Is there an option? Maybe. To construct a regular expression, you need to clearly define what it is you want to match and what you do not. Following are the rules defining the valid combinations in each number of an IP address:

- Any one- or two-digit number.
- Any three-digit number beginning with 1.
- Any three-digit number beginning with 2 if the second digit is 0 through 4.
- Any three-digit number beginning with 25 if the third digit is 0 through 5.

When laid out sequentially like that, it becomes clear that there is indeed a pattern that can work. Here's the example:

Text

```
Pinging hog.forta.com [12.159.46.200]
with 32 bytes of data:
```

RegEx

```
(((25[0-5])|(2[0-4]\d)|(1\d{2})|(\d{1,2}))\.){3}
➥(((25[0-5])|(2[0-4]\d)|(1\d{2})|(\d{1,2}))))
```

Result

```
Pinging hog.forta.com [12.159.46.200]
with 32 bytes of data:
```

Analysis

The pattern obviously worked, but it does require explanation. What makes this pattern work is a series of nested subexpressions. We'll start with `(((25[0-5])|(2[0-4]\d)|` `(1\d{2})|(\d{1,2}))\.)`, a set of four nested subexpressions, and we'll look at them in reverse order. `(\d{1,2})` matches any one- or two-digit number or numbers 0 through 99. `(1\d{2})` matches any three-digit number starting with 1 (1 followed by any two digits), or numbers 100 through 199. `(2[0-4]\d)` matches numbers 200 through 249. `(25[0-5])` matches numbers 250 through 255. Each of these subexpressions is enclosed within another subexpression with an `|` between each (so that one of the four subexpressions has to match, not all). After the range of numbers comes `\.` to match `.`, and then the entire series (all the number options plus `\.`) is enclosed into yet another subexpression and repeated three times using `{3}`. Finally, the range of numbers is repeated (this time without the trailing `\.`) to match the final IP address number. By restricting each of the four numbers to values between 0 and 255, this pattern can indeed match valid IP addresses and reject invalid addresses.

It is worth noting that the more logical order for these four expressions (the way I explained them above) would not have worked. Consider the following:

Text

```
Pinging hog.forta.com [12.159.46.200]
with 32 bytes of data:
```

RegEx

```
((((\d{1,2})|(1\d{2})|(2[0-4]\d)|(25[0-5])))\.){3}
➥(((\d{1,2})|(1\d{2})|(2[0-4]\d)|(25[0-5])))
```

Result

```
Pinging hog.forta.com [12.159.46.20 0]
with 32 bytes of data:
```

Analysis

Notice that this time the final 0 wasn't matched. Why is this? Because patterns are evaluated from left to right, and so when there are four expressions, any of which can match, the first is tested first, then the second, and so on. As soon as any pattern matches, the other options aren't even tested. In this example `(\d{1,2})` matches 20 in final 200, so the other options (including the final one, `(25[0-5])`, which is what was needed here) weren't even evaluated.

> **Tip**
>
> Regular expressions like this one can look overwhelming. The key to understanding them is to dissect them, analyzing and understanding one subexpression at a time. Start from the inside and work outward rather than trying to read character by character from the beginning. It is a lot less complex than it looks.

Summary

Subexpressions are used to group parts of an expression together and are defined using (and). Common uses for subexpressions include being able to control exactly what gets repeated by the repetition metacharacters and properly defining OR conditions. Subexpressions may be nested, if needed.

Lesson 8

Using Backreferences

The previous lesson introduced subexpressions as a way to group characters into sets. A primary use of this type of grouping is to be able to properly control repeating pattern matches (as was demonstrated in that lesson). This lesson looks at the other important use of subexpressions—working with backreferences.

Understanding Backreferences

The best way to understand the need for backreferences is to look at an example. HTML developers use the header tags (`<h1>` through `<h6>`, with corresponding end tags) to define and format header text within Web pages. Suppose you needed to locate all header text, regardless of header level. Here's the example:

Text

```
<body>
<h1>Welcome to my Homepage</h1>
Content is divided into two sections:<br/>
<h2>SQL</h2>
Information about SQL.
<h2>RegEx</h2>
Information about Regular Expressions.
</body>
```

RegEx

```
<[hH]1>.*<\/[hH]1>
```

Result

```
<body>
<h1>Welcome to my Homepage</h1>
Content is divided into two sections:<br/>
<h2>SQL</h2>
```

```
Information about SQL.
<h2>RegEx</h2>
Information about Regular Expressions.
</body>
```

Analysis

The pattern `<[hH]1>.*<\/[hH]1>` matched the first header (from `<h1>` until `</h1>`) and would also match `<H1>` (as HTML is not case sensitive). But what pattern could be used to match *any* header (which may be using any of the six valid header levels)?

One option would be to use a simple range instead of 1, like this:

Text

```
<body>
<h1>Welcome to my Homepage</h1>
Content is divided into two sections:<br/>
<h2>SQL</h2>
Information about SQL.
<h2>RegEx</h2>
Information about Regular Expressions.
</body>
```

RegEx

```
<[hH][1-6]>.*?<\/[hH][1-6]>
```

Result

```
<body>
<h1>Welcome to my Homepage</h1>
Content is divided into two sections:<br/>
<h2>SQL</h2>
Information about SQL.
<h2>RegEx</h2>
Information about Regular Expressions.
</body>
```

Analysis

That seemed to work; `<[hH][1-6]>` matches any header start tag (`<h1>` and `<h2>` in this example), and `<\/[hH][1-6]>` matches any header end tag (`</h1>` and `</h2>`).

Note

Notice that `.*?` (lazy) was used here, and not `.*` (greedy). As explained in Lesson 5, "Repeating Matches," quantifiers such as `*` are greedy, and so pattern `<[hH][1-6]>.*<\/ [hH][1-6]>` could match all the way from the opening `<h1>` on the second line until the closing `</h2>` on the sixth line. Using the lazy quantifier `.*?` instead solves this problem.

I said *could*, and not *would*, because this specific example would probably have worked even with the greedy quantifier. Metacharacter `.` usually does not match line breaks, and in the example, each header is on its own line. But there is no downside to using the lazy quantifier here, and so better safe than sorry.

Success? Not exactly. Look at the following example (using the same pattern):

Text

```
<body>
<h1>Welcome to my Homepage</h1>
Content is divided into two sections:<br/>
<h2>SQL</h2>
Information about SQL.
<h2>RegEx</h2>
Information about Regular Expressions.
<h2>This is not valid HTML</h3>
</body>
```

RegEx

```
<[hH][1-6]>.*?<\/[hH][1-6]>
```

Result

```
<body>
<h1>Welcome to my Homepage</h1>
Content is divided into two sections:<br/>
<h2>SQL</h2>
Information about SQL.
<h2>RegEx</h2>
Information about Regular Expressions.
<h2>This is not valid HTML</h3>
</body>
```

Analysis

A header tag starting with `<h2>` and ending with `</h3>` is invalid, and yet the pattern used here matched it.

The problem is that the second part of the match (the part matching the end tag) has no knowledge of the first part of the match (the part matching the start tag). And this is where backreferences become very useful.

Matching with Backreferences

We'll revisit the header problem shortly. For now let's look at a simpler example, and one that cannot be solved at all without the use of backreferences.

Suppose that you had a block of text and wanted to locate all repeated words (typos, where the same word was mistakenly typed twice). Obviously, when searching for the second occurrence of a word, that word must be known. Backreferences allow regular expression patterns to refer to previous matches (in this case, the previously matched word).

The best way to understand this is to see it used, so here is some text containing three sets of repeated words, all of which need to be located:

Text

```
This is a block of of text,
several words here are are
repeated, and and they
should not be.
```

RegEx

```
[ ]+(\w+)[ ]+\1
```

Result

```
This is a block of of text,
several words here are are
repeated, and and they
should not be.
```

Analysis

The pattern apparently worked, but how did it work? [ ]+ matches one or more spaces, \w+ matches one or more alphanumeric characters, and [ ]+ then matches any trailing spaces. But notice that \w+ is enclosed within parentheses, making it a subexpression. This subexpression is not used for repeating matches; there is no repeat matching here. Rather, the subexpression is used simply to group an expression, to flag it and identify it for future use. The final part of this pattern is \1; this is a reference back to the subexpression, \1 matches the same text as the first matched group. So when (\w+) matched the word of, so did \1, and when (\w+) matched the word and, so did \1.

Note

The term *backreference* refers to the fact that these entities *refer back* to a previous expression.

What exactly does \1 mean? It matches the first subexpression used in the pattern. \2 would match the second subexpression, \3 the third, and so on. [ ]+(\w+)[ ]+\1 thus matches any word and then the same word again as was seen in the preceding example.

Caution

Unfortunately, backreference syntax differs greatly from one regex implementation to another.

JavaScript used \ to denote a backreference (except in replace operations where $ is used), as does vi. Perl uses $ (so $1 instead of \1). The .NET regular expression support returns an object containing a property named Groups that contains the matches, so match.Groups[1] refers to the first match in C# and match.Groups(1) refers to that same match in Visual Basic .NET. PHP returns this information in an array named $matches, so $matches[1] refers to the first match (although this behavior can be changed based on the flags used). Java and Python return a match object containing an array named group.

Implementation specifics are listed in Appendix A.

Tip

You can think of backreferences as similar to variables.

Now that you've seen how backreferences are used, let's revisit the HTML header example. Using backreferences, it is possible to create a pattern that matches any header start tag and the matching end tag (ignoring any mismatched pairs). Here's the example:

Text

```
<body>
<h1>Welcome to my Homepage</h1>
Content is divided into two sections:<br/>
<h2>SQL</h2>
Information about SQL.
<h2>RegEx</h2>
Information about Regular Expressions.
<h2>This is not valid HTML</h3>
</body>
```

RegEx

```
<[hH]([1-6])>.*?<\/[hH]\1>
```

Result

```
<body>
<h1>Welcome to my Homepage</h1>
Content is divided into two sections:<br/>
<h2>SQL</h2>
Information about SQL.
<h2>RegEx</h2>
Information about Regular Expressions.
<h2>This is not valid HTML</h3>
</body>
```

Analysis

Again, three matches were found: one `<h1>` pair and two `<h2>` pairs. Like before, `<[hH]([1-6])>` matches any header start tag. But unlike before, `[1-6]` is enclosed within `(` and `)` so as to make it a subexpression. This way, the header end tag pattern can refer to that subexpression as `\1` in `<\/[hH]\1>`. `([1-6])` is a subexpression that matches digits `1` through `6`, and `\1` therefore matches only that same digit. This way, `<h2>This is not valid HTML</h3>` did not match.

> **Caution**
>
> Backreferences will work only if the expression to be referred to is a subexpression (and enclosed as such).

> **Tip**
>
> Matches are usually referred to starting with `1`. In many implementations, match `0` can be used to refer to the entire expression.

> **Note**
>
> As you have seen, subexpressions are referred to by their relative positions: `\1` for first, `\5` for fifth, and so on. Although commonly supported, this syntax does have one serious limitation: moving or editing subexpressions (and thus altering the subexpression order) could break your pattern, and adding or deleting subexpressions can be even more problematic.
>
> To address this shortcoming, some newer regular expression implementations support *named capture*, a feature whereby each subexpression may be given a unique name that may subsequently be used to refer to the subexpression (instead of the relative position). Named capture is not covered in this book because it is still not widely supported, and the syntax varies significantly between those implementations that do support it. However, if your implementation supports the use of named capture (.NET, for example), you should definitely take advantage of the functionality.

Performing Replace Operations

Every regular expression seen thus far in this book has been used for searching—locating text within a larger block of text. Indeed, it is likely that most of the regex patterns that you will write will be used for text searching. But that is not all that regular expressions can do; regular expressions can also be used to perform powerful replace operations.

Simple text replacements do not need regular expressions. For example, replacing all instances of CA with California and MI with Michigan is decidedly not a job for regular expressions. Although such a regex operation would be legal, there is no value in doing so, and in fact, the process would be easier (and would execute faster) using whatever regular string manipulation functions are available to you.

Regex replace operations become compelling when backreferences are used. The following is an example used previously in Lesson 5, "Repeating Matches":

Text

```
Hello, ben@forta.com is my email address.
```

RegEx

```
\w+[\w\.]*@[\w\.]+\.\w+
```

Result

Hello, ben@forta.com is my email address.

Analysis

This pattern identifies email addresses within a block of text (as explained back in Lesson 5).

But what if you wanted to make any email addresses in the text linkable? In HTML you would use `<a href="mailto:user@address.com">user@address.com</a>` to create a clickable email address. Could a regular expression convert an address to this clickable address format? Actually, yes, and very easily, too (as long as you are using backreferences):

Text

```
Hello, ben@forta.com is my email address.
```

RegEx

```
(\w+[\w\.]*@[\w\.]+\.\w+)
```

Replace

```
<a href="mailto:$1">$1</a>
```

Result

```
Hello, <a href="mailto:ben@forta.com">ben@forta.com</a>
is my email address.
```

Analysis

In replace operations, two regular expressions are used: one to specify the search pattern and a second to specify what to replace matched text with. Backreferences may span patterns, so a subexpression matched in the first pattern may be used in the second pattern. `(\w+[\w\.]*@[\w\.]+\.\w+)` is the same pattern used previously (to locate an email address), but this time it is specified as a subexpression. This way the matched text may be used in the replace pattern. `<a href="mailto:$1">$1</a>` uses the matched subexpression twice—once in the `href` attribute (to define the `mailto:`) and the other as the clickable text. So, `ben@forta.com` becomes `<a href="mailto:ben@forta.com">ben@forta.com</a>`, which is exactly what was wanted.

> **Caution**
>
> As noted previously, you will need to modify the backreference designator based on the implementation used. For example, JavaScript users will need to use $ instead of the previously used \.

> **Tip**
>
> As seen in this example, a subexpression may be referred to multiple times simply by referring to the backreference as needed.

Let's look at one more example. User information is stored in a database, and phone numbers are stored in the format `313-555-1234`. However, you need to reformat the phone numbers as `(313) 555-1234`. Here is the example:

Text

```
313-555-1234
248-555-9999
810-555-9000
```

RegEx

```
(\d{3})(-)(\d{3})(-)(\d{4})
```

Replace

```
($1) $3-$5
```

Result

```
(313) 555-1234
(248) 555-9999
(810) 555-9000
```

Analysis

Again, two regular expression patterns are used here. The first looks far more complicated than it is, so let's walk through it. `(\d{3})(-)(\d{3})(-)(\d{4})` matches a phone number, but breaks it into five subexpressions (so as to isolate its parts). `(\d{3})` matches the first three digits as the first subexpression, `(-)` matches – as the second subexpression, and so on. The end result is that the phone number is broken into five parts (each part its own subexpression): the area code, a hyphen, the first three digits of the number, another hyphen, and then the final four digits. These five parts can be used individually and as needed, and so `($1) $3-$5` simply reformats the number using only three of the subexpressions and ignoring the other two, thereby turning `313-555-1234` into `(313) 555-1234`.

> **Tip**
>
> When manipulating text for reformatting, it is often useful to break the text into lots of little subexpressions so as to have greater control over that text.

Converting Case

Some RegEx implementations support the use of conversion operations via the metacharacters listed in Table 8.1.

Table 8.1   **Case Conversion Metacharacters**

Metacharacter	Description
\E	Terminate \L or \U conversion
\l	Convert next character to lowercase
\L	Convert all characters up to \E to lowercase
\u	Convert next character to uppercase
\U	Convert all characters up to \E to uppercase

`\l` and `\u` are placed before a character (or expression) so as to convert the case of the next character. `\L` and `\U` convert the case of all characters until a terminating `\E` is reached.

Following is a simple example, converting the text within an `<h1>` tag pair to uppercase:

Text

```
<body>
<h1>Welcome to my Homepage</h1>
Content is divided into two sections:<br/>
<h2>SQL</h2>
Information about SQL.
<h2>RegEx</h2>
Information about Regular Expressions.
<h2>This is not valid HTML</h3>
</body>
```

RegEx

```
(<[Hh]1>)(.*?)(<\/[Hh]1>)
```

Replace

```
$1\U$2\E$3
```

Result

```
<body>
<h1>WELCOME TO MY HOMEPAGE</h1>
Content is divided into two sections:<br/>
<h2>SQL</h2>
Information about SQL.
<h2>RegEx</h2>
Information about Regular Expressions.
<h2>This is not valid HTML</h3>
</body>
```

Analysis

The pattern `(<[Hh]1>)(.*?)(<\/[Hh]1>)` breaks the header into three subexpressions: the opening tag, the text, and the closing tag. The second pattern then puts the text back together: `$1` contains the start tag, `\U$2\E` converts the second subexpression (the header text) to uppercase, and `$3` contains the end tag.

Summary

Subexpressions are used to define sets of characters or expressions. In addition to being used for repeating matches (as seen in the previous lesson), subexpressions can be referred to within patterns. This type of reference is called a backreference (and unfortunately, there are implementation differences in backreference syntax). Backreferences are useful in text matching and in replace operations.

Lesson 9
Looking Ahead and Behind

All the expressions used thus far have matched text, but sometimes you may want to use expressions to mark the position of text to be matched (in contrast to the matched text itself). This involves the use of *lookaround* (the capability to look ahead and behind), which will be explained in this lesson.

Introducing Lookaround

Again, we'll start with an example. You need to extract the title of a Web page; HTML page titles are placed between `<title>` and `</title>` tags in the `<head>` section of HTML code. Here's the example:

Text

```
<head>
<title>Ben Forta's Homepage</title>
</head>
```

RegEx

```
<[tT][iI][tT][lL][eE]>.*<\/[tT][iI][tT][lL][eE]>
```

Result

```
<head>
<title>Ben Forta's Homepage</title>
</head>
```

Analysis

`<[tT][iI][tT][lL][eE]>.*<\/[tT][iI][tT][lL][eE]>` matches the opening `<title>` tag (in upper, lower, or mixed case), the closing `</title>` tag, and whatever text is between them. That worked.

Or did it? What you needed was the title text, but what you got also contained the opening and closing `<title>` tags. Is it possible to return just the title text?

One solution could be to use subexpressions (as seen in Lesson 7, "Using Subexpressions"). This would allow for you to retrieve the matched text in three parts—the opening tag, the text, and the closing tag—and with the matched text broken into parts, it would not be too difficult to extract just that part you want.

But it makes little sense to make the effort to retrieve something that you actually don't want, only to have to manually remove it. What you really need here is a way to construct a pattern so that it contains matches that are not returned—matches that are used so as to find the correct match location, but not used as part of the core match. In other words, you need to *look around*.

> **Note**
>
> This lesson discusses both *lookahead* and *lookbehind*. The former is supported in all major regular expression implementations, but the latter is not supported as extensively.
>
> Java, .NET, PHP, Python, and Perl all support lookbehind (some with restrictions). JavaScript, however, does not.

Looking Ahead

Lookahead specifies a pattern to be matched but not returned. A lookahead is actually a subexpression and is formatted as such. The syntax for a lookahead pattern is a subexpression preceded by `?=`, and the text to match follows the `=` sign.

> **Tip**
>
> Some regular expression documentation uses the term *consume* to refer to what is matched and returned; lookahead matches are said to *not consume*.

Here is an example. The following text contains a list of URLs, and you need to extract the protocol portion of each (possibly so as to know how to process them):

Text

```
http://www.forta.com/
https://mail.forta.com/
ftp://ftp.forta.com/
```

RegEx

```
.+(?=:)
```

Result

```
http://www.forta.com/
https://mail.forta.com/
ftp://ftp.forta.com/
```

Analysis

In the URLs listed, the protocol is separated from the hostname by a :. Pattern .+ matches any text (http in the first match), and subexpression (?=:) matches :. But notice that the : was not matched; ?= tells the regular expression engine to match : but to look ahead (and not consume it).

To better understand what ?= is doing, here is the same example, this time without the lookahead metacharacters:

Text

```
http://www.forta.com/
https://mail.forta.com/
ftp://ftp.forta.com/
```

RegEx

```
.+(:)
```

Result

```
http://www.forta.com/
https://mail.forta.com/
ftp://ftp.forta.com/
```

Analysis

The subexpression (:) correctly matches :, but the matched text is consumed and is returned as part of the match.

The difference between the two examples is that the former used pattern (?=:) to match the :, and the latter used (:). Both of these patterns matched the same thing; they both matched the : after the protocol. The difference is in whether that matched : was actually included in the matched text. When using lookahead, the regular expression parser looks ahead to process the : match, but does not process it as part of the primary search. .+(:) finds the text up to and including the :. .+(?=:) finds the text up to, but not including, the :.

> **Note**
>
> Lookahead (and lookbehind) matches actually do return results, but the results are always 0 characters in length. As such, you will sometimes find the lookaround operations referred to as being *zero-width*.

> **Tip**
>
> Any subexpression can be turned into a lookahead expression by simply prefacing the text with ?=. Multiple lookahead expressions may be used in a search pattern, and they may appear anywhere in the pattern (not just at the beginning, as shown here).

Looking Behind

As you have just seen, ?= looks ahead (it looks at what comes after the matched text, but does not consume what it finds). ?= is thus referred to as the *lookahead* operator. In addition to looking ahead, many regular expression implementations support looking behind. Looking at what is before the text to be returned involves looking behind, and the *lookbehind* operator ?<=.

> **Tip**
>
> Need help distinguishing ?= and ?<= from each other? Here's a way to remember which is which: the one that contains the arrow pointing behind (the < character) is **lookbehind**.

?<= is used in the same way as ?=; it is used within a subexpression and is followed by the text to match.

Following is an example. A database search lists products, and you need only the prices:

Text

```
ABC01: $23.45
HGG42: $5.31
CFMX1: $899.00
XTC99: $69.96
Total items found: 4
```

RegEx

```
\$[0-9.]+
```

Result

```
ABC01: $23.45
HGG42: $5.31
CFMX1: $899.00
XTC99: $69.96
Total items found: 4
```

Analysis

\$ matches the $, and [0-9.]+ matches the price.

That worked. But what if you did not want the $ characters in the matched text? Could you simply drop \$ from the pattern?:

Text

```
ABC01: $23.45
HGG42: $5.31
CFMX1: $899.00
XTC99: $69.96
Total items found: 4
```

RegEx

```
[0-9.]+
```

Result

```
ABC01: $23.45
HGG42: $5.31
CFMX1: $899.00
XTC99: $69.96
Total items found: 4
```

Analysis

That obviously did not work. You do need the \$ so as to determine which text to match, but you do not want the $ to be returned.

The solution? A lookbehind match, as follows:

Text

```
ABC01: $23.45
HGG42: $5.31
CFMX1: $899.00
XTC99: $69.96
Total items found: 4
```

RegEx

```
(?<=\$)[0-9.]+
```

Result

```
ABC01: $23.45
HGG42: $5.31
CFMX1: $899.00
XTC99: $69.96
Total items found: 4
```

Analysis

That did the trick. (?<=\$) matches $, but does not consume it, and so only the prices (without the leading $ signs) are returned.

Compare the first and last expressions used in this example. `\$[0-9.]+` matched $ followed by a dollar amount. `(?<=\$)[0-9.]+` also matched $ followed by a dollar amount. The difference between the two is not in what they located while performing the search, but in what they included in the results. The former located and included the $. The latter located $ so as to correctly find the prices, but did not include that $ in the matched results.

> **Caution**
>
> Lookahead patterns may be variable length; they may contain . and +, for example, so as to be highly dynamic.
>
> Lookbehind patterns, on the other hand, must generally be fixed length. This is a restriction imposed by almost all regular expression implementations.

Combining Lookahead and Lookbehind

Lookahead and lookbehind operations may be combined, as in the following example (the solution to the problem at the start of this lesson):

Text

```
<head>
<title>Ben Forta's Homepage</title>
</head>
```

RegEx

```
+
```

Result

```
<head>
<title>Ben Forta's Homepage</title>
</head>
```

Analysis

That worked. `(?<=<[tT][iI][tT][lL][eE]>)` is a lookbehind operation that matches (but does not consume) `<title>`; `(?=</[tT][iI][tT][lL][eE]>)` similarly matches (but does not consume) `</title>`. All that is returned is the title text (as that is all that was consumed).

> **Tip**
>
> In the preceding example, it may be worthwhile to escape the < (the first character being matched) to prevent ambiguity, so `(?<=\<` instead of `(?<=<`.

Negating Lookaround

As seen thus far, lookahead and lookbehind are usually used to match text, essentially to specify the location of text to be returned (by specifying the text before or after the desired match). These are known as *positive lookahead* and *positive lookbehind*. The term *positive* refers to the fact that they look for a match.

A lesser-used form of lookaround is the *negative* lookaround. *Negative lookahead* looks ahead for text that does *not* match the specified pattern, and *negative lookbehind* similarly looks behind for text that does *not* match the specified pattern.

You might have expected to be able to use ^ to negate a lookaround, but no, the syntax is a little different. Lookaround operations are negated using ! (which replaces the =). Table 9.1 lists all the lookaround operations.

Table 9.1   **Lookaround Operations**

Class	Description
(?=)	Positive lookahead
(?!)	Negative lookahead
(?<=)	Positive lookbehind
(?<!)	Negative lookbehind

Tip

Generally, any regular expression implementations supporting lookahead support both positive and negative lookahead. Similarly, those implementations supporting lookbehind support both positive and negative lookbehind.

To demonstrate the difference between positive and negative lookbehind, here is an example. The following block of text contains numbers—both prices and quantities. First we'll just obtain the prices:

Text

```
I paid $30 for 100 apples,
50 oranges, and 60 pears.
I saved $5 on this order.
```

RegEx

```
(?<=\$)\d+
```

Result

```
I paid $30 for 100 apples,
50 oranges, and 60 pears.
I saved $5 on this order.
```

Analysis

This is very similar to the example seen previously. \d+ matches numbers (one or more digits), and (?<=\$) looks behind to match (but not consume) the $ (escaped as \$). Therefore, the numbers in the two prices were matched, but not the quantities.

Now we'll do the opposite, locating just the quantities but not the prices:

Text

```
I paid $30 for 100 apples,
50 oranges, and 60 pears.
I saved $5 on this order.
```

RegEx

```
\b(?<!\$)\d+\b
```

Result

```
I paid $30 for 100 apples,
50 oranges, and 60 pears.
I saved $5 on this order.
```

Analysis

Again, \d+ matched numbers, but this time only the quantities were matched and not the prices. Expression (?<!\$) is a negative lookbehind that will match only when what precedes the numbers is not a $. Changing the = in the lookbehind changes the pattern from positive to negative.

You may be wondering why the pattern in the negative lookbehind example defines word boundaries (using \b). To understand why this is necessary, here is the same example without those boundaries:

Text

```
I paid $30 for 100 apples,
50 oranges, and 60 pears.
I saved $5 on this order.
```

RegEx

```
(?<!\$)\d+
```

Result

```
I paid $30 for 100 apples,
50 oranges, and 60 pears.
I saved $5 on this order.
```

Analysis

Without word boundaries, the 0 in $30 was also matched. Why? Because there is $ in front of it. Enclosing the entire pattern within word boundaries solves this problem.

Summary

Looking ahead and behind provides greater control over what is returned when matches are made. The lookaround operations allow subexpressions to be used to specify the location of text to be matched but not consumed (matched, but not included in the matched text itself). Positive lookahead is defined using (?=), and negative lookahead is defined using (?!). Some regular expression implementations also support lookbehind using (?<=) and negative lookahead using (?<!).

Lesson 10

Embedding Conditions

A powerful yet infrequently used feature of the regular expression language is the capability to embed conditional processing within an expression. This lesson will explore this topic.

Why Embed Conditions?

(123)456-7890 and 123-456-7890 are both acceptable presentation formats for North American phone numbers. 1234567890, (123)-456-7890, and (123-456-7890 all contain the correct number of digits, but are badly formatted. How could you write a regular expression to match only the *acceptable* formats and not any others?

This is not a trivial problem; consider this obvious solution:

Text

```
123-456-7890
(123)456-7890
(123)-456-7890
(123-456-7890
1234567890
123 456 7890
```

RegEx

```
\(?\d{3}\)?-?\d{3}-\d{4}
```

Result

```
123-456-7890
(123)456-7890
(123)-456-7890
(123-456-7890
1234567890
123 456 7890
```

Analysis

`\(?` matches an optional opening parenthesis (notice that `(` must be escaped), `\d{3}` matches the first three digits, `\)?` matches an optional closing parenthesis, `-?` matches an optional hyphen, and `\d{3}-\d{4}` match the remaining seven digits (separated by a hyphen). The pattern correctly did not match the last two lines, but it did match the third and fourth—both of which are incorrect (the third contains both `)` and `-`, and the fourth has an unmatched parenthesis).

Replacing `\)?-?` with `[\)-]?` will help eliminate the third line (by allowing only `)` or `-`, but not both) but the fourth line is a problem. The pattern needs to match `)` only if there is an opening `(`. In truth, the pattern needs to match `)` if there is an opening `(`. If not, it needs to match `-`, and that type of pattern cannot be implemented without conditional processing.

> **Caution**
> Conditional processing is not supported by all regular expression implementations.

Using Conditions

Regular expression conditions are defined using `?`. In fact, you have already seen a couple of very specific conditions:

- `?` matches the previous character or expression *if* it exists.

- `?=` and `?<=` match text ahead or behind, *if* it exists.

Embedded condition syntax also uses `?`, which is not surprising considering that the conditions that are embedded are the same two just listed:

- Conditional processing based on a backreference.

- Conditional processing based on lookaround.

Backreference Conditions

A backreference condition allows for an expression to be used only if a previous subexpression search was successful. If that sounds obscure, consider an example: you need to locate all `<img>` tags in your text; in addition, if any `<img>` tags are links (enclosed between `<a>` and `</a>` tags), you need to match the complete link tags as well.

The syntax for this type of condition is `(?(backreference)true)`. The `?` starts the condition, the backreference is specified within parentheses, and the expression to be evaluated only if the backreference is present immediately follows.

Now for the example:

Text

```
<!-- Nav bar -->
<div>
<a href="/home"><img src="/images/home.gif"></a>
<img src="/images/spacer.gif">
<a href="/search"><img src="/images/search.gif"></a>
<img src="/images/spacer.gif">
<a href="/help"><img src="/images/help.gif"></a>
</div>
```

RegEx

```
(<[Aa]\s+[^>]+>\s*)?<[Ii][Mm][Gg]\s+[^>]+>(?(1)\s*<\/[Aa]>)
```

Result

```
<!-- Nav bar -->
<div>
<a href="/home"><img src="/images/home.gif"></a>
<img src="/images/spacer.gif">
<a href="/search"><img src="/images/search.gif"></a>
<img src="/images/spacer.gif">
<a href="/help"><img src="/images/help.gif"></a>
</div>
```

Analysis

This pattern requires explanation. `(<[Aa]\s+[^>]+>\s*)?` matches an opening `<A>` or `<a>` tag (with any attributes that may be present), if present (the closing `?` makes the expression optional). `<[Ii][Mm][Gg]\s+[^>]+>` then matches the `<img>` tag (regardless of case) with any of its attributes. `(?(1)\s*</[Aa]>)` starts off with a condition: `?(1)` means execute only what comes next if backreference `1` (the opening `<A>` tag) exists (or in other words, execute only what comes next if the first `<A>` match was successful). If `(1)` exists, then `\s*<\/[Aa]>` matches any trailing whitespace followed by the closing `</A>` tag.

> **Note**
>
> `?(1)` checks to see if backreference `1` exists. The backreference number (`1` in this example) does not need to be escaped in conditions. So, `?(1)` is correct, and `?(\1)` is not (although the latter will usually work, too).

The pattern just used executes an expression if a condition is met. Conditions can also have *else* expressions, expressions that are executed only if the backreference does not exist (the condition is not met). The syntax for this form of condition is `(?(backreference)true|false)`. This syntax accepts a condition, as well as the expressions to be executed if the condition is met or not met.

This syntax provides the solution for the phone number problem as shown here:

Text

```
123-456-7890
(123)456-7890
(123)-456-7890
(123-456-7890
1234567890
123 456 7890
```

RegEx

```
(\()?\d{3}(?(1)\)|-)\d{3}-\d{4}
```

Result

```
123-456-7890
(123)456-7890
(123)-456-7890
(123-456-7890
1234567890
123 456 7890
```

Analysis

This pattern seemed to work, but why? As before, `(\()?` checks for the start of a parentheses pair, but this time the results are enclosed within parentheses so as to be able to create a subexpression. `\d{3}` matches the three-digit area code. `(?(1)\)|-)` matches either `)` or `-` depending on whether the condition is satisfied. If `(1)` exists (meaning that an open parenthesis was found), then `\)` must be matched; otherwise, `-` must be matched. This way, parentheses must always be paired, and the hyphen separating the area code from the number is matched only if parentheses are not used. Why did the fourth line match? Because the opening `(` has no matching pair it is assumed to be unrelated text and is ignored altogether.

> **Tip**
>
> Patterns can start to look very complex when conditions are embedded, and this can make troubleshooting very difficult. It is generally a good idea to build and test small parts of the expression and then put them together.

Lookaround Conditions

A lookaround condition allows for expressions to be executed based on whether a lookahead or lookbehind operation succeeded. The syntax for lookaround conditions is much the same as it is for backreference conditions, except that the backreference (the number inside of the parentheses) is replaced by a complete lookaround expression.

> **Note**
> Refer to Lesson 9, "Looking Ahead and Behind," for details on using lookaround processing.

As an example, consider U.S. ZIP codes. These may be five-digit ZIP codes formatted as `12345` or ZIP+4 codes formatted as `12345-6789`. The hyphen is used only if the additional four digits are present. Here's one solution:

Text

```
11111
22222
33333-
44444-4444
```

RegEx

```
\d{5}(-\d{4})?
```

Result

```
11111
22222
33333-
44444-4444
```

Analysis

`\d{5}` matches the first five digits, and `(-\d{4})?` matches a hyphen followed by four more digits if they all exist.

But what if you wanted to not match any badly formatted ZIP codes? The third line in the example has a trailing hyphen that probably should not be there. The preceding pattern matched the digits without the hyphen, but how could you not match that entire ZIP code because it is badly formatted?

This example may seem a bit contrived, but it does simply demonstrate the use of lookaround conditions. So:

Text

```
11111
22222
33333-
44444-4444
```

RegEx

```
\d{5}(?(?=-)-\d{4})
```

Result

```
11111
22222
33333-
44444-4444
```

Analysis

Again, \d{5} matches the opening five digits. Then comes a condition in the form of (?(?=-)-\d{4}). The condition uses lookahead ?=- to match (but not consume) a hyphen, and if the condition is met (the hyphen exists), then -\d{4} matches that hyphen followed by four digits. This way, 33333- is not matched (it has a hyphen and so the condition is met, but it does not have the additional four digits).

Lookahead and lookbehind (both positive and negative) may be used as the condition, and an optional *else* expression may be used, too (using the same syntax seen previously, |expression).

Tip

Lookaround conditions tend not to be used frequently because similar results can often be accomplished using simpler means.

Summary

Conditions may be embedded into regular expression patterns so as to be able to execute expressions only if a condition has (or has not) been met. The condition may be a backreference (the condition is then checking for its existence) or a lookaround operation.

Lesson 11

Regular Expression Solutions to Common Problems

This lesson is a collection of useful regular expressions, along with detailed explanations of each. The intent is to both summarize everything you have learned in this book by using practical real-world examples and give you a leg up by providing commonly needed patterns that you can use.

> **Note**
>
> The examples presented here are not the ultimate solutions to the problems presented. By now it should be clear that there rarely is an ultimate solution. More often, multiple solutions exist with varying degrees of tolerance for the unpredictable, and there is always a trade-off between performance of a pattern and its capability to handle any and all scenarios thrown at it. With that understanding, feel free to use the patterns presented here (and if needed, tweak them as suits you best).

North American Phone Numbers

The North American Numbering Plan defines how North American telephone numbers are formatted. As per the plan, telephone numbers (in the U.S., Canada, much of the Caribbean, and several other locations) are made up of a three-digit area code (technically, the NPA or *numbering plan area*) and then a seven-digit number (which is formatted as a three-digit *prefix* followed by a hyphen and a four-digit *line number*). Any digits may be used in a phone number with two exceptions: the first digit of the area code and the first digit of the prefix may not be 0 or 1. The area code is often enclosed within parentheses, and the area code is often separated from the actual phone number by a hyphen. Matching one of (555) 555-5555 or (555)555-5555 or 555-555-5555 is easy; matching any of them (assuming that that is what you need) is a bit trickier.

Text

J. Doe: 248-555-1234
B. Smith: (313) 555-1234
A. Lee: (810)555-1234

RegEx

`\(?[2-9]\d\d\)?[ -]?[2-9]\d\d-\d{4}`

Result

J. Doe: 248-555-1234
B. Smith: (313) 555-1234
A. Lee: (810)555-1234

Analysis

The pattern begins with the curious-looking `\(?`. Parentheses are optional, `\(` matches `(`, and `?` matches 0 or 1 instance of that `(`. `[2-9]\d\d` matches a three-digit area code (the first digit must be 2 through 9). `\)?` matches the optional closing parenthesis. `[ -]?` matches a single space or a hyphen, if either of them exist. `[2-9]\d\d-\d{4}` matches the rest of the phone number, the three-digit prefix (the first digit of which must be 2 through 9), followed by a hyphen and four more digits.

This pattern could easily be modified to handle other presentation formats. For example, `555.555.5555`:

Text

J. Doe: 248-555-1234
B. Smith: (313) 555-1234
A. Lee: (810)555-1234
M. Jones: 734.555.9999

RegEx

`[\(.]?[2-9]\d\d[\).]?[ -]?[2-9]\d\d[-.]\d{4}`

Result

J. Doe: 248-555-1234
B. Smith: (313) 555-1234
A. Lee: (810)555-1234
M. Jones: 734.555.9999

Analysis

The opening match now tests for `(` or `.` as an optional set, using pattern `[\(.]?`. Similarly, `[\).]?` tests for `)` or `.` (also both optional), and `[-.]` tests for `-` or `.`. Other phone number formats could be added just as easily.

U.S. ZIP Codes

ZIP codes were introduced to the U.S. in 1963 (ZIP is actually an acronym for *Zone Improvement Plan*). There are more than 40,000 U.S. ZIP codes, all made up of digits (the first digit is assigned from East to West, with 0 being on the East Coast and 9 being on the West Coast). In 1983, the post office began using an expanded ZIP code called *ZIP+4*. The extra four digits provide a greater level of granularity (often a specific city block or sometimes a specific building), which in turn provides for greater mail reliability. Use of ZIP+4 is optional, and as such, ZIP-code validation usually must be able to accommodate both five-digit ZIP codes and ZIP+4 (with a hyphen separating the first five digits from the additional four digits):

Text

```
999 1st Avenue, Bigtown, NY, 11222
123 High Street, Any City, MI 48034-1234
```

RegEx

```
\d{5}(-\d{4})?
```

Result

```
999 1st Avenue, Bigtown, NY, 11222
123 High Street, Any City, MI 48034-1234
```

Analysis

\d{5} matches any five digits, and -\d{4} matches a hyphen followed by the +4 digits. Because these additional four digits are essentially optional, -\d{4} is enclosed within parentheses (turning it into a subexpression), and ? is used to optionally allow a single instance of that subexpression.

Canadian Postal Codes

Canadian postal codes are six characters made up of alternating letters and digits. The first series of three letters and digits identify the *forward sortation area* (or FSA), and the second series of three letters and digits identify the *local delivery unit* (or LDU). The first letter of the FSA identifies the province, territory, or region (18 letters are valid in this position, A for Newfoundland and Labrador, B for Nova Scotia, K, L, N, and P for Ontario, excluding Toronto, which uses M, and so on), and so validation should ideally check to ensure that the first letter is a valid one. Canadian postal codes are generally formatted using a space to separate the FSA from the LDU:

Text

```
123 4th Street, Toronto, Ontario, M1A 1A1
567 8th Avenue, Montreal, Quebec, H9Z 9Z9
```

RegEx

```
[ABCEGHJKLMNPRSTVXY]\d[A-Z] \d[A-Z]\d
```

Result

```
123 4th Street, Toronto, Ontario, M1A 1A1
567 8th Avenue, Montreal, Quebec, H9Z 9Z9
```

Analysis

[ABCEGHJKLMNPRSTVXY] matches any one of those 18 valid characters, and \d[A-Z] matches a digit followed by any alphabetic character, and thus the FSA. \d[A-Z]\d matches the LDU, a digit followed by an alphabetic character followed by a digit.

> **Note**
>
> This regular expression is one that should not be case sensitive.

United Kingdom Postcodes

United Kingdom postcodes are five, six, or seven letters and digits defined by the Royal Mail. Postcodes are made up of two parts: the outward postcode (or *outcode*) and the inward postcode (or *incode*). The outcode is one or two alphabetic letters followed by one or two digits, or one or two letters followed by a digit and a letter. The incode is always a single digit followed by two characters (any characters excluding C, I, K, M, O, and V, which are never used in postcodes). The incode and outcode are separated by a space:

Text

```
171 Kyverdale Road, London N16 6PS
33 Main Street, Portsmouth, PO1 3AX
18 High Street, London NW11 8AB
```

RegEx

```
[A-Z]{1,2}\d[A-Z\d]? \d[ABD-HJLNP-UW-Z]{2}
```

Result

```
171 Kyverdale Road, London N16 6PS
33 Main Street, Portsmouth, PO1 3AX
18 High Street, London NW11 8AB
```

Analysis

The incode first matches one or two alphabetic characters followed by a digit using `[A-Z]{1,2}\d`. `[A-Z\d]?` matches an additional alphanumeric character if it exists. As such, `[A-Z]{1,2}\d[A-Z\d]?` matches every possible valid incode combination. To match the outcode, the pattern `\d[ABD-HJLNP-UW-Z]{2}` is used; this matches a single digit followed by two of the allowed alphabetic characters (A, B, D through H, J, L, N, P through U, and W through Z).

> **Note**
>
> This regular expression is one that should not be case sensitive.

U.S. Social Security Numbers

U.S. social security numbers (often abbreviates to SSN) are three sets of digits separated by hyphens; the first set contains three digits, the second set contains two digits, and the third set contains four digits. Since 1972, the first set of three digits have been assigned based on the address provided on the application:

Text

```
John Smith: 123-45-6789
```

RegEx

```
\d{3}-\d{2}-\d{4}
```

Result

John Smith: `123-45-6789`

Analysis

`\d{3}-\d{2}-\d{4}` matches any three digits followed by a hyphen, two digits, a hyphen, and any four digits.

> **Note**
>
> Most combinations of digits are potentially valid social security numbers, but a couple of rules can be used if needed. Valid social security numbers will never have a field that is all 0s, and the first set of digits (thus far) must be no greater than 728 (numbers higher than that have never been assigned yet, although they could be at some time in the future). However, this would be a very complex pattern to write, and so the simpler `\d{3}-\d{2}-\d{4}` is usually used.

IP Addresses

IP addresses are made up of four bytes (each with a valid range of 0-255). IP addresses are usually formatted as four sets of digits (each is one to three digits in length) separated by . characters:

Text

```
localhost is 127.0.0.1.
```

RegEx

```
(((25[0-5])|(2[0-4]\d)|(1\d{2})|(\d{1,2}))\.){3}
➡(((25[0-5])|(2[0-4]\d)|(1\d{2})|(\d{1,2})))
```

Result

```
localhost is 127.0.0.1.
```

Analysis

This pattern uses a series of nested subexpressions. `(((25[0-5])|(2[0-4]\d)|(1\d{2})|(\d{1,2}))\.)` is a set of four nested subexpressions. `(\d{1,2})` matches any one- or two-digit number or numbers 0 through 99. `(1\d{2})` matches any three-digit number starting with 1 (1 followed by any two digits), or numbers 100 through 199. `(2[0-4]\d)` matches numbers 200 through 249. `(25[0-5])` matches numbers 250 through 255. Each of these subexpressions is enclosed within another subexpression with a | between each (so that one of the four subexpressions has to match, not all). After the range of numbers comes `\.` to match ., and then the entire series (all the number options plus `\.`) is enclosed into yet another subexpression and repeated three times using {3}. Finally, the range of numbers is repeated (this time without the trailing `\.`) to match the final IP address number. By restricting each of the four numbers to values between 0 and 255, this pattern can indeed match valid IP addresses and reject invalid addresses.

> **Note**
>
> This IP address example is explained in detail in Lesson 7, "Using Subexpressions."

URLs

URL matching is a complicated task—or rather, it can be complicated depending on how flexible the matching needs to be. At a minimum, URL matching should match the protocol (probably http and https), a hostname, an optional port, and a path:

Text

```
http://www.forta.com/blog
https://www.forta.com:80/blog/index.cfm
http://www.forta.com
http://ben:password@www.forta.com/
http://localhost/index.php?ab=1&c=2
http://localhost:8500/
```

RegEx

```
https?:\/\/[-\w.]+(:\d+)?(\/([\w\/_.]*)?)?
```

Result

```
http://www.forta.com/blog
https://www.forta.com:80/blog/index.cfm
http://www.forta.com
http://ben:password@www.forta.com/
http://localhost/index.php?ab=1&c=2
http://localhost:8500/
```

Analysis

`https?://` matches `http://` or `https://` (the `?` makes the `s` optional). `[-\w.]+` matches the hostname. `(:\d+)?` matches an optional port (as seen in the second and sixth lines in the example). `(/([\w/_.]*)?)?` matches the path, the outer subexpression matches `/` if one exists, and the inner subexpression matches the path itself. As you can see, this pattern cannot handle query strings, and it misreads embedded username:password pairs. However, for most URLs it will work adequately (matching hostnames, ports, and paths).

> **Note**
>
> This regular expression is one that should not be case sensitive.

> **Tip**
>
> To accept ftp URLs as well, replace the https? with `(http|https|ftp)`. You can do the same for other URL types if needed.

Complete URLs

A more complete (and slower) pattern would also match URL query strings (variable information passed to a URL and separated from the URL itself by a ?), as well as optional user login information, if specified:

Text

```
http://www.forta.com/blog
https://www.forta.com:80/blog/index.cfm
http://www.forta.com
http://ben:password@www.forta.com/
http://localhost/index.php?ab=1&c=2
http://localhost:8500/
```

RegEx

```
https?:\/\/(\w*:\w*@)?[-\w.]+(:\d+)?(\/([\w\/_.]*(\?\S+)?)?)?
```

Result

```
http://www.forta.com/blog
https://www.forta.com:80/blog/index.cfm
http://www.forta.com
http://ben:password@www.forta.com/
http://localhost/index.php?ab=1&c=2
http://localhost:8500/
```

Analysis

This pattern builds on the previous example. `https?://` is now followed by `(\w*:\w*@)?`. This new pattern checks for embedded user and password (username and password separated by `:` and followed by `@`) as seen in the fourth line in the example. In addition, `(\?\S+)?` (after the path) matches the query string, `?` followed by additional text, and this, too, is made optional with `?`.

> **Note**
> This regular expression is one that should not be case sensitive.

> **Tip**
> Why not always use this pattern over the previous one? In performance, this is a slightly more complex pattern and so it will run slower; if the extra functionality is not needed it should not be used.

Email Addresses

Regular expressions are frequently used for email address validation, and yet validating a simple email address is anything but simple:

Text

```
My name is Ben Forta, and my
email address is ben@forta.com.
```

RegEx

`(\w+\.)*\w+@(\w+\.)+[A-Za-z]+`

Result

My name is Ben Forta, and my
email address is ben@forta.com.

Analysis

`(\w+\.)*\w+` matches the name portion of an email address (everything before the @). `(\w+\.)*` matches zero or more instances of text followed by `.`, and `\w+` matches required text (this combination matches both `ben` and `ben.forta`, for example). `@` matches @. `(\w+\.)+` then matches at least one instance of text followed by `.`, and `[A-Za-z]+` matches the top-level domain (`com` or `edu` or `us` or `uk`, and so on).

The rules governing valid email address formats are extremely complex. This pattern will not validate every possible email address. For example, it will allow `ben..forta@forta.com` (which is invalid) and will not allow IP addresses as the hostname (which are allowed). Still, it will suffice for most email validation, and so it may work for you.

> **Note**
>
> Regular expressions used to match email addresses should usually not be case sensitive.

HTML Comments

Comments in HTML pages are placed between `<!--` and `-->` tags (use at least two hyphens, although more are allowed). Being able to locate all comments is useful when browsing (and debugging) Web pages:

Text

```
<!-- Start of page -->
<html>
<!-- Start of head -->
<head>
<tile>My Title</title> <!-- Page title -->
</head>
<!-- Body -->
<body>
```

RegEx

`<!-{2,}.*?-{2,}>`

Result

```
<!-- Start of page -->
<html>
<!-- Start of head -->
<head>
<tile>My Title</title> <!-- Page title -->
</head>
<!-- Body -->
<body>
```

Analysis

`<!-{2,}` matches the start of the comment, `<!` followed by two or more hyphens. `.*?` matches the comment body (not greedy). `-{2,}>` matches the end of the comment.

> **Note**
>
> This regular expression matches two or more hyphens and can thus be used to find CFML comments, too (which are identified by three hyphens). However, the pattern does not attempt to match the number of hyphens at the comment's start and close (potentially a useful enhancement in finding mismatched comments).

JavaScript Comments

Comments in JavaScript (and in other scripting languages, including ActionScript and other ECMAScript derivatives) are preceded by //. As in the previous example, being able to locate all comments in a page at once can be very useful:

Text

```
<script language="JavaScript">
// Turn off fields used only by replace
function hideReplaceFields() {
  document.getElementById('RegExReplace').disabled=true;
  document.getElementById('replaceheader').disabled=true;
}
// Turn on fields used only by replace
function showReplaceFields() {
  document.getElementById('RegExReplace').disabled=false;
  document.getElementById('replaceheader').disabled=false;
}
```

RegEx

```
\/\/.*
```

Result

```
<script language="JavaScript">
// Turn off fields used only by replace
function hideReplaceFields() {
  document.getElementById('RegExReplace').disabled=true;
  document.getElementById('replaceheader').disabled=true;
}
// Turn on fields used only by replace
function showReplaceFields() {
  document.getElementById('RegExReplace').disabled=false;
  document.getElementById('replaceheader').disabled=false;
}
```

Analysis

This is a simple one; \/\/.* matches // followed by the comment body.

Credit Card Numbers

Credit card numbers cannot be truly validated using regular expressions; final validation always requires some interaction with a credit card processing organization. However, regular expression validation can indeed be useful in trapping typos (like one digit too many or too few) before submitting any data anywhere.

> **Note**
>
> The patterns used here all assume that any embedded spaces or hyphens have been removed. This is generally a good practice to remove any nondigits from credit card numbers before performing any regular expression processing.

All credit cards follow a basic numbering scheme—an opening digit sequence followed by a specified number of digits. We'll start with MasterCard:

Text

```
MasterCard: 5212345678901234
Visa 1: 4123456789012
Visa 2: 4123456789012345
Amex: 371234567890123
Discover: 601112345678901234
Diners Club: 38812345678901
```

RegEx

```
5[1-5]\d{14}
```

Result

```
MasterCard: 5212345678901234
Visa 1: 4123456789012
Visa 2: 4123456789012345
Amex: 371234567890123
Discover: 601112345678901234
Diners Club: 38812345678901
```

Analysis

All MasterCard numbers are 16 digits; the first digit is always 5, and the second digit is 1 through 5. 5[1-5] matches the first two digits; \d{14} matches the next 14 digits.

Visa is a little trickier:

Text

```
MasterCard: 5212345678901234
Visa 1: 4123456789012
Visa 2: 4123456789012345
Amex: 371234567890123
Discover: 601112345678901234
Diners Club: 38812345678901
```

RegEx

```
4\d{12}(\d{3})?
```

Result

```
MasterCard: 5212345678901234
Visa 1: 4123456789012
Visa 2: 4123456789012345
Amex: 371234567890123
Discover: 601112345678901234
Diners Club: 38812345678901
```

Analysis

All Visa numbers start with 4 and are 13 or 16 digits (but not 14 or 15, and so a range cannot be used). 4 matches 4, \d{12} matches the next 12 digits, and (\d{3})? matches an additional 3 digits if they are present.

American Express requires a much simpler pattern:

Text

```
MasterCard: 5212345678901234
Visa 1: 4123456789012
```

```
Visa 2: 4123456789012345
Amex: 371234567890123
Discover: 601112345678901234
Diners Club: 38812345678901
```

RegEx

```
3[47]\d{13}
```

Result

```
MasterCard: 5212345678901234
Visa 1: 4123456789012
Visa 2: 4123456789012345
Amex: 371234567890123
Discover: 601112345678901234
Diners Club: 38812345678901
```

Analysis

American Express numbers are 15 digits and start with 34 or 37. 3[47] matches the first 2 digits, and \d{13} matches the remaining 13 digits.

Discover also uses a simple pattern:

Text

```
MasterCard: 5212345678901234
Visa 1: 4123456789012
Visa 2: 4123456789012345
Amex: 371234567890123
Discover: 601112345678901234
Diners Club: 38812345678901
```

RegEx

```
6011\d{14}
```

Result

```
MasterCard: 5212345678901234
Visa 1: 4123456789012
Visa 2: 4123456789012345
Amex: 371234567890123
Discover: 601112345678901234
Diners Club: 38812345678901
```

Analysis

All Discover cards are 16 digits and start with digits `6011`; `6011\d{14}` does the trick.

Diners Club is a little trickier:

Text

```
MasterCard: 5212345678901234
Visa 1: 4123456789012
Visa 2: 4123456789012345
Amex: 371234567890123
Discover: 601112345678901234
Diners Club: 38812345678901
```

RegEx

```
(30[0-5]|36\d|38\d)\d{11}
```

Result

```
MasterCard: 5212345678901234
Visa 1: 4123456789012
Visa 2: 4123456789012345
Amex: 371234567890123
Discover: 601112345678901234
Diners Club: 38812345678901
```

Analysis

Diners Club numbers are 14 digits and begin with `300` through `305`, `36`, or `38`. If the opening digits are `300` through `305`, an additional 11 digits are needed, whereas if the opening digits are `36` or `38`, an additional 12 digits are needed. To make this simpler, the pattern first matches the first three digits regardless of what they are. `(30[0-5]|36\d|38\d)` has three expressions, any of which must match; `30[0-5]` matches `300` through `305`, `36\d` matches any three-digit number starting with `36`, and `38\d` matches any three-digit number starting with `38`. This way, `\d{11}` can be used to match the remaining 11 digits.

All that remains now is a way to check any of the five card types used here:

Text

```
MasterCard: 5212345678901234
Visa 1: 4123456789012
Visa 2: 4123456789012345
Amex: 371234567890123
Discover: 601112345678901234
Diners Club: 38812345678901
```

RegEx

```
(5[1-5]\d{14})|(4\d{12}(\d{3})?)|(3[47]\d{13})|
➡(6011\d{14})|((30[0-5]|36\d|38\d)\d{11})
```

Result

```
MasterCard: 5212345678901234
Visa 1: 4123456789012
Visa 2: 4123456789012345
Amex: 371234567890123
Discover: 601112345678901234
Diners Club: 38812345678901
```

Analysis

The pattern here uses alternation (providing alternatives, *or* statements) to include all the previous patterns, each separated by a |. The result? Simple validation of all major credit card types.

> **Note**
>
> The patterns used here ensure that the credit card number has the correct opening digits and is of the correct length. However, not every 13-digit number that begins with 4 is a valid Visa number. A formula known as *Mod 10* can be used to perform a calculation on the digits (of all the credit card types mentioned here) so as to determine if the digits are truly valid. Mod 10 is an important part of implementing credit card processing, but it is not a job for regular expressions because it involves performing mathematical calculations.

Summary

You have now seen practical examples of many of the concepts and ideas introduced in prior lessons. Feel free to use, and adapt, any of the examples used here; with that, welcome to the exciting and productive world of regular expressions.

Appendix A

Regular Expressions in Popular Applications and Languages

Although basic regular expression syntax is, for the most part, consistent across different implementations, the way that regular expressions are used is most definitely not. Languages and applications that support regular expression use have their invocation methods, and most have their own subtle (and sometimes not so subtle) differences and nuances. This appendix describes regular expression use in popular applications and languages and provides additional usage notes where appropriate.

> **Note**
>
> The information presented in this appendix is for reference and to help you get started. Specific usage examples and notes for every implementation are beyond the scope of this book, and you should refer to the relevant application or language documentation for further information.

grep

grep is the Unix utility used to perform text searches against files or standard input text. grep supports basic, extended, and Perl regular expressions, depending on the option specified:

- -E uses extended regular expressions.
- -G uses basic regular expressions.
- -P uses Perl regular expressions.

> **Tip**
>
> Exact features and functionality vary based on the option specified. Most users opt for Perl regular expressions (described later) because these are the most standard.

Note the following:

- By default, grep displays the entire line for any lines containing matches; to show just the match, use the -o option.

- Use option -v to negate the match and display only nonmatching lines.

- Use option -c to display the count (number of matches) instead of all match details.

- Use option -i for matching that is not case sensitive.

- grep is used for search operations, not for replace operations. As such, no replace functionality is supported.

Java

Regular expression matching is facilitated via the java.util.rgex.matcher class and these methods:

- find() finds an occurrence of a pattern within a string.

- lookingAt() attempts to match the start of a string against a specified pattern.

- matches() attempts to match an entire string against a specified pattern.

- replaceAll() performs a replace operation and replaces all matches.

- replaceFirst() performs a replace operation and replaces the first match.

Additional class methods provide greater control over specific operations. In addition, simple wrapper methods are available in the java.util.regex.pattern class:

- compile() compiles a regular expression into a pattern.

- flags() returns a pattern's match flags.

- matches() is functionally equivalent to the matches() method described earlier.

- pattern() returns the regular expression from which a pattern was created.

- split() splits a string into substrings.

Sun's regular expression support is based on the Perl implementation, but be aware of the following:

- To use regular expressions, the regular expression package must be imported using import java.util.regex.*. (This will include the entire package. If only subsets of the package are needed, specify their names instead of *.)

- Embedded conditions are not supported.

- Case conversion using \E, \l, \L, \u, and \U is not supported.

- Backspace matching via \b is not supported.

- \z is not supported.

JavaScript

JavaScript implements regular expression processing in the `String` and `RegEx` objects via the following methods:

- `exec` is a `RegEx` method used to search for a match.
- `match` is a `String` method used to match a string.
- `replace` is a `String` method used to perform replace operations.
- `search` is a `String` method used to test for a match in a string.
- `split` is a `String` method used to break a string into multiple strings.
- `test` is a `RegEx` method used to test for a match in a string.

JavaScript regular expression support is modeled on that of Perl, but be aware of the following:

- JavaScript uses flags to manage global case-sensitive searching: `g` enables global, `i` makes matches not case sensitive, and the two flags may be combined as `gi`.
- Additional modifiers (supported by later than version 4 browsers) are `m` to support multiline strings, `s` for single-line strings, and `x` to ignore whitespace within the regex pattern.
- When you use backreferences, `$`` returns everything before the matched string, `$'` returns everything after the matched string, `$+` returns the last matched subexpression, and `$&` returns everything that matched.
- JavaScript features a global object named `RegExp`, which can be accessed to obtain information about the execution after a regular expression has been executed.
- The POSIX character classes are not supported.
- `\A` and `\Z` are not supported.

Microsoft .NET

The .NET Framework provides powerful and flexible regular-expression processing as part of the base class library. As such, regular expressions are available for use by any .NET languages and tools (including ASP.NET, C#, and Visual Studio .NET).

Regular expression support in .NET is provided by the `Regex` class (as well as additional supporting classes). `Regex` includes the following methods:

- `IsMatch()` checks to see whether a match is found in a specified string.
- `Match()` searches for a single match, which is returned as a `Match` object.
- `Matches()` searches for all matches, which are returned as a `MatchCollection` object.
- `Replace()` performs a replace operation on a specified string.
- `Split()` splits a string into an array of strings.

It is also possible, via wrapper functions, to execute a regular expression without needing to instantiate and work with a Regex class instance:

- `Regex.IsMatch()` is functionally equivalent to the `IsMatch()` method described in the previous list.

- `Regex.Match()` is functionally equivalent to the `Match()` method.

- `Regex.Matches()` is functionally equivalent to the `Matches()` method.

- `Regex.Replace()` is functionally equivalent to the `Replace()` method.

- `Regex.Split()` is functionally equivalent to the `Split()` method.

Here are some important points pertaining to .NET regular expression support:

- To use regular expressions, the regular expression objects must be imported using `Imports System.Text.RegularExpressions`.

- For quick inline regular expression processing, the wrapper functions are ideal.

- Regular expression options are specified using the `Regex.Options` property—a `RegexOption` enumeration that can be used to set members such as `IgnoreCase`, `Multiline`, `Singleline`, and more.

- .NET supports named capture, the capability to name subexpressions (so as to be able to refer to them by name instead of number). The syntax for this is `?<name>` to name a subexpression, `\k<name>` to refer to the backreference, and `${name}` to refer to it in a replacement pattern.

- When using backreferences, `$`` returns everything before the matched string, `$'` returns everything after the matched string, `$+` returns the last matched subexpression, `$_` returns the entire original string, and `$&` returns the entire matched string.

- Case conversion using `\E`, `\l`, `\L`, `\u`, and `\U` is not supported.

- The POSIX character classes are not supported.

Microsoft SQL Server T-SQL

Microsoft SQL Server does not support regular expressions natively. However, SQL Server T-SQL statements can use the Microsoft CLR (Common Language Runtime), which does expose regular expression functionality. CLR is beyond the scope of this book, but documentation can be found on the Microsoft site.

Microsoft Visual Studio .NET

Regular expression support in Visual Studio .NET is provided by the .NET Framework. See the .NET section earlier in this appendix.

To use regular expressions, do the following:

- Select Find and Replace from the Edit menu.
- Select Find, Replace, Find in Files, or Replace in Files.
- Check the Use check box, and select Regular expressions from the drop-down list.

Note the following:

- Use @ instead of *?.
- Use # instead of +?.
- Use ^n instead of {n}.
- In replace operations, backreferences may be padded so as to be left justified by using \(w,n) (where w is the width, and n is the backreference). To right justify, use \(-w,n).
- Visual Studio .NET uses the following special metacharacters and symbols: :a for [a-zA-Z0-9], :c for [a-zA-Z], :d for \d, :h for [a-fA-F0-9] (hexadecimal characters), :i for valid identifiers [a-zA-Z_$][a-zA-Z_0-9$]*, :q for a quoted string, :w for [a-zA-Z]+, :z for \d+.
- \n is a platform-independent line-break character and inserts a new line when used in replace operations.
- The following special letter matching characters are supported: :Lu matches any uppercase letter, :Ll matches any lowercase letter, :Lt matches title case (first letter capitalized), :Lm matches punctuation characters.
- The following special numeric matching characters are supported: :Nd for [0-9]+, :Nl for Roman numerals.
- The following special punctuation matching characters are supported: :Ps for punctuation openings, :Pe for punctuation closings, :Pi for double quotation marks, :Pf for single quotation marks, :Pd for a dash (hyphen), :Pc for underscore, :Po for other punctuation characters.
- The following special symbol matching characters are supported: :Sm for mathematical symbols, :Sc for currency symbols, :Sk for accent modifiers, :So for other special symbols.
- Other special characters are supported, too; consult the Visual Studio .NET documentation for more details.

MySQL

MySQL is a popular open source database, and MySQL ventures where no other databases have yet to venture by providing regular expression support as a way to perform database searches.

Regular expression support in MySQL is accessed in WHERE clauses in the following format:

```
REGEXP "expression"
```

> **Note**
> A complete MySQL statement using a regular expression would use syntax like this:
> `SELECT * FROM table WHERE REGEXP "pattern"`.

MySQL regular expression support is useful and powerful, but it is not a full regular expression implementation:

- Only search support is provided; there is no support for replace operations.
- Searches are not case sensitive. To perform case-sensitive searches, use the `BINARY` keyword (between `REGEXP` and the expression itself).
- Use `[[:<:]]` to match the start of a word and `[[:>:]]` to match the end of a word.
- Lookaround is not supported.
- Embedded conditions are not supported.
- Octal character searching is not supported.
- `\a`, `\b`, `\e`, `\f`, and `\v` are not supported.
- Backreferences are not supported.

Oracle PL/SQL

PL/SQL is the SQL format used in Oracle DBMSs. PL/SQL supports regular expressions as follows:

- `REGEXP_LIKE` can be used in lieu of SQL `LIKE`.

Following are some useful notes pertaining to PL/SQL regular expressions:

- `REGEXP_LIKE` can be used to match text in `VARCHAR2`, `CHAR`, `NVARCHAR2`, `NCHAR`, `CLOB`, or `NCLOB` data types.
- Specify `REGEXP_LIKE` match parameter c for case-sensitive matching.
- Specify `REGEXP_LIKE` match parameter i for case-insensitive matching.
- Specify `REGEXP_LIKE` match parameter n to allow . to match the newline character.
- Specify `REGEXP_LIKE` match parameter x to ignore whitespace characters.
- The pipe character | can be used for OR.

Perl

Perl is the granddaddy of regular expression implementations, and most other implementations attempt to be Perl compatible.

Regular expression support is a core part of Perl and is used simply by specifying the operation and the pattern:

- `m/pattern/` matches the specified pattern.
- `s/pattern/pattern/` performs a replace operation.
- `qr/pattern/` returns a `Regex` object that may be used later.
- `split()` splits a string into substrings.

Following are some useful notes pertaining to Perl regular expressions:

- Modifiers may be passed after the pattern. Use `/i` for searching that is not case sensitive and `/g` for global (match all matches).
- When you use backreferences, `$`` returns everything before the matched string, `$'` returns everything after the matched string, `$+` returns the last matched subexpression, and `$&` returns the entire matched string.

PHP

PHP provides Perl-compatible regular expression support via the PCRE (Perl Compatible Regular Expressions) package.

The following regular expression functions are supported by PCRE:

- `preg_grep()` performs a search and returns an array of matches.
- `preg_match()` performs a regular expression search for the first match.
- `preg_match_all()` performs a global regular expression search.
- `preg_quote()` takes a pattern and returns an escaped version of it.
- `preg_replace()` performs a search-and-replace operation.
- `preg_replace_callback()` performs a search-and-replace operation, but uses a callback function to perform the actual replacement.
- `preg_split()` splits a string into substrings.

Note the following:

- For matching that is not case sensitive, use the `i` modifier.
- Multiline strings can be enabled using the `m` modifier.
- PHP can evaluate replacement strings as PHP code. To enable this functionality, use the `e` modifier.
- `preg_replace()`, `preg_replace_callback()`, and `preg_split()` all support an optional parameter that specifies a limit—the maximum number of replacements or splits to be performed.

- Backreferences may be referred to using Perl $ syntax ($1, for example) in PHP 4.0.4 or later; earlier versions use \\ instead of $.

- \1, \u, \L, \U, \E, \Q, and \v are not supported.

Python

Python provides regular expression support via the re module.

The following regular expression functions are supported by Python:

- preg_grep() performs a search and returns an array of matches.

- findall() finds all substrings and returns them as a list.

- finditer() finds all substrings and returns them as an iterator.

- match() performs a regular expression search on the start of a string.

- search() performs a search for all matches in a string.

- split() converts a string into a list, splitting it wherever the pattern matches.

- sub() replaces matches with a specified substring.

- subn() returns a string in which matches are replaced with a specified substring.

Note the following:

- Before they can be used, regular expressions are compiled into objects using re.compile.

- re.compile accepts optional flags like re.IGNORECASE for case-insensitive searching.

- Use flag re.VERBOSE to help with regular expression debugging.

- match() and search() return None if no matches are found.

Index

N

Accessing the Free Web Edition

Your purchase of this book in any format includes access to the corresponding Web Edition, which provides several special online-only features:

- The complete text of the book

- Links to online regular expression testers

- Updates and corrections as they become available

The Web Edition can be viewed on all types of computers and mobile devices with any modern web browser that supports HTML5.

To get access to the *Learning Regular Expressions* Web Edition all you need to do is register this book:

1. Go to www.informit.com/register.

2. Sign in or create a new account.

3. Enter the ISBN: 9780134757063.

4. Answer the questions as proof of purchase.

5. The Web Edition will appear under the Digital Purchases tab on your Account page. Click the Launch link to access the product.